Power Shifts and New Blocs in the Global Trading System

Edited by

Sanjaya Baru and Suvi Dogra

Power Shifts and New Blocs in the Global Trading System

Edited by

Sanjaya Baru and Suvi Dogra

IISS The International Institute for Strategic Studies

The International Institute for Strategic Studies

Arundel House | 13–15 Arundel Street | Temple Place | London | WC2R 3DX | UK

First published February 2015 **Routledge**
4 Park Square, Milton Park, Abingdon, Oxon, OX14 4RN

for **The International Institute for Strategic Studies**
Arundel House, 13–15 Arundel Street, Temple Place, London, WC2R 3DX, UK
www.iiss.org

Simultaneously published in the USA and Canada by **Routledge**
270 Madison Ave., New York, NY 10016

Routledge is an imprint of Taylor & Francis, an Informa Business

© 2015 The International Institute for Strategic Studies

DIRECTOR-GENERAL AND CHIEF EXECUTIVE Dr John Chipman
EDITOR Dr Nicholas Redman
EDITORIAL MANAGER Nancy Turner
ASSISTANT EDITOR Sarah Johnstone
EDITORIAL Jill Lally, Anna Ashton
COVER/PRODUCTION John Buck, Kelly Verity
COVER IMAGE Shutterstock

The International Institute for Strategic Studies is an independent centre for research, information and debate on the problems of conflict, however caused, that have, or potentially have, an important military content. The Council and Staff of the Institute are international and its membership is drawn from almost 100 countries. The Institute is independent and it alone decides what activities to conduct. It owes no allegiance to any government, any group of governments or any political or other organisation. The IISS stresses rigorous research with a forward-looking policy orientation and places particular emphasis on bringing new perspectives to the strategic debate.

The Institute's publications are designed to meet the needs of a wider audience than its own membership and are available on subscription, by mail order and in good bookshops. Further details at www.iiss.org.

Printed and bound in Great Britain by Bell & Bain Ltd, Thornliebank, Glasgow

British Library Cataloguing in Publication Data
A catalogue record for this book is available from the British Library

Library of Congress Cataloging in Publication Data

ADELPHI series
ISSN 1944-5571

ADELPHI 450
ISBN 978-1-138-92724-7

Contents

ACKNOWLEDGEMENTS

Many of the chapters in this book are derived from papers delivered at a conference on 'Trade and Flag: The Changing Balance of Power in the Multilateral Trade System', organised by the IISS Geo-economics and Strategy Programme and held at the IISS–Middle East offices, in Manama, Bahrain, in April 2014, with the support of the Bahrain Development Board. For more on the conference, please visit http://www.iiss.org/en/events/geo-economics-s-seminars/trade-and-flag-256b.

Opinions expressed in these articles are the authors' and do not necessarily reflect those of their employers.

CONTRIBUTORS

Braz Baracuhy	Consulting Senior Fellow for Geo-economics and Strategy, IISS, and diplomat serving in the Brazilian Foreign Ministry's policy planning staff.
Sanjaya Baru	Director for Geo-economics and Strategy, IISS, and Honorary Senior Fellow, Centre for Policy Research, New Delhi.
Jagdish Bhagwati	Professor of Law and Economics at Columbia University and Senior Fellow at the Council on Foreign Relations. He has served in top-level advisory positions for the WTO and the UN, including as Economic Policy Adviser to the Director-General of the General Agreement on Tariffs and Trade (GATT) from 1991–93.
Suvi Dogra	Research and Liaison Officer for the Geo-economics and Strategy Programme, IISS.
Pravin Krishna	Chung Ju Yung Distinguished Professor of International Economics and Business at Johns Hopkins University. He is also a Research Associate at the National Bureau of Economic Research (NBER).
Pascal Lamy	French political adviser and Honorary President of Paris-based think tank Notre Europe, Lamy was the Director-General of the World Trade Organisation (WTO) from 2005–13. He is also a former European Commissioner for Trade.
Arvind Panagariya	Vice-Chair of the National Institution for Transforming India Aayog (NITI Aayog), an Indian government think tank. Professor of Economics at Columbia University, Panagariya is also an ex-Chief Economist at the Asian Development Bank.

Supachai Panitchpakdi Secretary-General of the United Nations Conference on Trade and Development (UNCTAD) from 2005–13 and Director-General of the WTO from 2002–05.

Arvind Subramanian Chief Economic Adviser to the government of Indian Prime Minister Narendra Modi, Subramanian previously held senior fellowships at the Peterson Institute for International Economics and the Center for Global Development.

Ashley J. Tellis Senior Associate at the Carnegie Endowment for International Peace specialising in international security, defence and Asian strategic issues. Previously, he served in the US Foreign Service and on the National Security Council staff as Special Assistant to the President and Senior Director for Strategic Planning and Southwest Asia.

GLOSSARY

APEC   Asia-Pacific Economic Cooperation – a forum of 21 countries with a Pacific coastline: Australia, Brunei, Canada, Chile, China, Hong Kong (China), Indonesia, Japan, Korea, Malaysia, Mexico, New Zealand, Papua New Guinea, Peru, the Philippines, Russia, Singapore, Taiwan (China), Thailand, the United States and Vietnam.

ASEAN   Association of Southeast Asian Nations – a bloc of ten countries: Brunei, Cambodia, Indonesia, Laos, Malaysia, Myanmar, the Philippines, Singapore, Thailand and Vietnam. ASEAN has a population of more than 600 million, combined GDP of US$2.4 trillion (2013 IMF figures) and 6.8% of world trade (2012 WTO figures).

DDA   Doha Development Agenda, the name for the Doha Round of multilateral trade negotiations preferred by developing countries and acknowledged by WTO headquarters as the round's 'semi-official' title. Many commentators mix the two names, by referring to the Doha Development Round.

GATT   General Agreement on Tariffs and Trade (GATT) – a provisional deal and organisation signed by 23 countries in 1947 and governing the international trade in goods from 1 January 1948 until the launch of its successor, the WTO (see below) in 1995. By that time, 123 countries had acceded to the agreement.

ISDS   Investor–State Dispute Settlement – a public international law provision under which foreign investors can sue host countries for acting in a way (through laws and policies) that damages an investor's interests. ISDS is found in many trade treaties.

RCEP   Regional Comprehensive Economic Partnership – a free-trade deal being negotiated between ASEAN (see above) and the six countries with which it already has free-trade agreements

– Australia, China, India, Japan, Korea and New Zealand. Participants have a total population of more than 3 billion, combined GDP of around US$21trn (2013 figures) and an estimated trade share of around 27% of global trade (2012 figures).

TPP Trans-Pacific Partnership – a 'mega-regional' trade agreement to bring together the US, Australia, Brunei, Canada, Chile, Japan, Malaysia, Mexico, New Zealand, Peru, Singapore and Vietnam. These countries have a population in excess of 800m, combined GDP of about US$28trn, or 40% of global GDP (2012 figures), and account for roughly one-third of world trade.

TTIP Transatlantic Trade and Investment Partnership – a free-trade area being sought between the US and EU (total population 850m). As the partners together represent 60% of global GDP, 33% of world trade in goods and 42% of world trade in services (2012 figures), it would be the largest bilateral free-trade deal in history.

WTO World Trade Organisation – with 160 members at the start of 2015 (and the Seychelles to become the 161st), the WTO is the body now responsible for setting and administering the rules of global trade, including those already established during the GATT years.

Power shifts and new blocs in global trade

Sanjaya Baru

Reflecting on the challenges facing the World Trade Organisation (WTO), and its inability to conclude the Doha Development Round of multilateral trade negotiations, the then-director-general of the WTO, Pascal Lamy, suggested to an audience in Melbourne in November 2012 that the 'rising weight of influence of emerging economies has shifted the balance of power' in the global trading system, and that there has been a 'redistribution of the geopolitical deck of cards on a global scale'.[1] The impact of this change in the balance of power in world trade became the focus of the WTO's annual publication, the *World Trade Report 2013*.[2]

Lamy and the *WTR 2013* were both highlighting the sharp rise in the share of world trade of the emerging economies, most importantly the new global 'trading power' China, and the growing clout of these countries in WTO negotiations, thanks in part to their growing domestic markets for goods and services. One consequence of this structural change in the cross-border flows of merchandise goods and services has been an increase in trade between developing countries. This means that, using terms popularised by development economists in the 1970s, a long-standing pattern of 'north–south' trade, or trade between the 'centre' and the 'periphery', has been changed by increased 'south–south' trade.

Taken together these two trends, namely, the rise of a new trading power and increased south–south trade, have not only altered global trade flows but have also contributed to a shift in the negotiating power of developing countries within the WTO. Yet, while trade economists have written extensively on the changing dynamics of global trade, the geopolitics of these economic shifts has not received much attention. As Nobel Prize-winning economist Thomas C. Schelling observed long ago, 'Aside from war and preparations for war, and occasionally aside from migration, trade is the most important relationship that most countries have with each other … trade policy is national security policy.'[3]

At the time of its creation in the mid-1990s, the WTO was shaped by the geo-economic consequences of the end of the Cold War and the rise of non-Western economies, especially in East Asia. Developing countries were able to institutionalise their newly acquired geo-economic clout by influencing the principles of decision-making in the WTO. Yet, the struggle for power between the developed and developing economies continues. The impasse in the first round of trade negotiations being conducted by the WTO, namely that begun in Doha in 2001, symbolises this continuing conflict. Indeed, nothing captures this better than a difference of opinion on the very name of the round. While many in the developed economies insist on referring to it as simply the Doha Round, representatives of the developing world insist on highlighting the 'development' in the Doha Development Agenda (DDA).

New trading powers, especially China, Brazil, India and South Africa, often complain that they have not been able to secure what they set out to at Doha, despite their growing economic weight. However, some believe they have succeeded in preventing the round from moving forward. There was an attempt to break the impasse at the WTO's Bali Ministerial Conference in December 2013, when ministers agreed to a text on trade facilitation. But India's insistence on securing changes in the Agreement on Agriculture, to protect its domestic food-security scheme, has once again raised questions about the future of the Doha negotiations.[4]

A second consequence of the 'power shift' in the global trading system has been an increase in policy activity aimed at constructing new plurilateral preferential and regional trade agreements (PTAs/RTAs). In the first year of his presidency, Barack Obama reaffirmed the United States' commitment to a nascent PTA initiative, the Trans-Pacific Partnership (TPP). The US followed this up by launching a Transatlantic Trade and Investment Partnership (TTIP) designed to build further bridges with the EU, which has also been concerned about China's emergence as a 'mega-trader'.

Supporters of the TPP and TTIP view these initiatives as either an attempt by some to break the deadlock in the WTO and move forward, or as an attempt to open a parallel 'high-speed' track on which countries seeking faster trade liberalisation can progress. Either way, these views present the TPP and TTIP as 'WTO-plus' initiatives – i.e., involving further integration in areas covered by the WTO such as industrial and agricultural tariffs, technical barriers to trade, intellectual property and public procurement. Critics of plurilateral preferential trade agreements, on the other hand, reject the view that they are in fact 'building blocks' of multilateralism and suggest they have become 'stumbling blocks'. Leading trade theorist Jagdish Bhagwati has been one of the most consistent critics of PTAs/RTAs, and in the co-authored essay in this volume he once again rebuffs the arguments in favour of the TPP, TTIP and all other such plurilateral arrangements, reiterating the importance of a globally open multilateral trading regime.

While trade economists debate the pros and cons of multilateralism and regionalism, geopolitical analysts take a different view of these policy initiatives. In a slim, stimulating volume on the geo-economics of China's rise,[5] Edward Luttwak, an early conceptualiser of the idea of 'geo-economics',[6] proposes that countries whose economies are under threat from China's policies – policies that seek to make China's industries globally more competitive – should come together to 'contain' China geo-economically.[7]

Are the TPP and TTIP aimed at the geo-economic containment of China? In his essay in this volume, Ashley J. Tellis discusses this possibility. While the post-war open trading regime, with its preferential treatment of developing countries, was in fact designed and implemented by the United States, the US itself is under geo-economic pressure from a rising new 'mega-trader', and Tellis says the time may have come for Washington to consider new ways of managing economic multilateralism. So, why have these 'mega-blocs' gained traction? Even Pascal Lamy, who takes a more sanguine view of the TPP and TTIP in his essay, concludes: 'Multilateralism has not been threatened by regionalism. But prospects for the future are more blurred.' Is this blurring a product of competing economic objectives or of conflicting political ones? Are new mega-RTAs such as the TPP and TTIP merely the 'building blocks' of a new multilateralism or a threat to it? Are these initiatives a testament to the failure of the WTO in ensuring trade openness or a political response by the West to the 'rise of the rest'?

The essays in this volume seek to answer these questions. The first two essays set the stage by defining the nature of the extant global economic and trading environment. Bhagwati,

Krishna and Panagariya pay tribute to the WTO for its contribution to trade liberalisation worldwide and underscore the importance of strengthening the multilateral system rather than weakening it. Subramanian analyses the economic and geopolitical consequences of the rise of China as the new global 'mega-trader'. Both Lamy and Panitchpakdi emphasise the importance of strengthening the WTO. However, Lamy is more understanding of the developed economies' impatience with the developing ones, while Panitchpakdi highlights disappointment with the lack of progress on the Doha Round's 'development' objectives.

The geopolitics of global trade, of the power shift from 'the West to the rest' and the options for the US in dealing with the rise of China are issues discussed in detail by Ashley J. Tellis. While urging US lawmakers and the administration to pursue policies that will ensure that the US regains its competitive advantage, Tellis sees nothing wrong in the US pursuing plurilateral initiatives that help it deal with the competition from China, and rejects the view that these amount to a 'geo-economic containment' of China.

While it is understandable that the US and EU would seek to preserve the twentieth-century order in which the economies of the West dominated and defined the rules of global trade, Baracuhy suggests that in the twenty-first century a 'multipolar geo-economic power structure' is in the making and that countries like Brazil, China, India and other emerging economies will matter far more as the processes of globalisation become more 'polycentric'. Will the West cede its hegemonic authority to accommodate a wider set of actors and states with different aspirations to govern the international system? This volume offers a balanced assessment of how the global power shift is impacting the rules of the global trading system.

Notes

1 Pascal Lamy, 'The Future of the Multilateral Trading System?', The Richard Snape Lecture, November 2012, Melbourne, Australia, http://www.wto.org/english/news_e/sppl_e/sppl258_e.htm.

2 *World Trade Report 2013 – Factors Shaping the Future of World Trade* (Geneva: World Trade Organisation, 2013).

3 T.C. Schelling, 'Testimony before the Williams Commission on United States International Economic Policy in an Interdependent World', vol. 1. p. 737, quoted in Richard N. Cooper, 'Trade Policy is Foreign Policy', *Foreign Policy*, no. 9, Winter 1972–73, p. 32.

4 India pulled out of a 2013 trade-facilitation agreement due to concerns over the WTO rule that caps subsidies to farmers in developing countries at 10% of the total value of agricultural production. Delhi was particularly concerned because the minimum support price it pays to farmers under a new US$4 billion-a-year scheme to supply cheap food to 800 million people could lead it to breach the 10% cap, and it sought assurances that this food-security scheme would be excluded from legal challenges under the WTO.

5 Edward Luttwak, *The Rise of China vs. The Logic of Strategy* (Cambridge, MA: The Belknap Press of Harvard University, 2012), p. 38.

6 Edward Luttwak, 'From Geopolitics to Geo-economics', *National Interest*, no. 20, Summer 1990.

7 Luttwak *The Rise of China vs. The Logic of Strategy*, p. 42.

CHAPTER ONE

Where is the world trade system heading?

Jagdish Bhagwati, Pravin Krishna and Arvind Panagariya

When the Uruguay Round of multilateral trade negotiations was successfully closed in 1994, and the General Agreement on Tariffs and Trade (GATT) metamorphosed into the World Trade Organisation (WTO), the despondency surrounding those protracted negotiations was replaced by euphoria. GATT had been an agreement on tariff reduction with an improvised set of rules governing trade in goods, rather than the stillborn International Trade Organisation (ITO) that was meant to sit alongside the International Monetary Fund (IMF) and the World Bank as the third pillar of the international economic super-structure formed after the Second World War.[1] On 1 January 1995, the WTO finally emerged as that missing institution.

A key function of the WTO is the implementation of exist-ing agreements among member countries. When the WTO replaced GATT, it greatly expanded sectoral coverage by bring-ing textiles, agriculture and services into the multilateral rule book.[2] It created a uniform intellectual property rights regime, and it replaced GATT's relatively weak dispute-settlement mechanism with a system that made dispute resolution virtu-ally binding on member governments.

But the failure of member countries to close the Doha Round of trade negotiations long after they were begun in 2001, and the proliferation of bilateral and plurilateral preferential trade arrangements (PTAs) involving Western nations since, has cast a shadow over the WTO's future. Some important successes were achieved at the WTO Ministerial Conference in Bali in December 2013, especially in improving trade facilitation, the reduction of trade barriers for imports from the least developed countries (LDCs) and shielding, on an interim basis, food-security programmes in developing countries. However, subsequent developments have raised fresh doubts about the future of the Doha Round.

There is much to celebrate about the WTO's achievements in creating a liberal trading system. Developing countries' enhanced participation in world trade is another significant achievement of the multilateral trading system. South–south trade flows have expanded substantially during the organisation's existence. There has also been a growing appreciation among the developing countries of the need to safeguard their trade interests, and they have accomplished this through more effective participation in the WTO. All in all, developing countries now represent a much greater share of the multilateral trade system and, importantly, constitute a new set of interests for the system to engage and accommodate.

Yet despite the successes of the multilateral process in expanding trade, it is readily evident that both developed and developing countries have systematically moved towards PTAs. Developed countries have also used the threat of proceeding on the bilateral track to bend the multilateral process in their preferred direction. As the then-United States Trade Representative (USTR) Susan Schwab pointedly noted in June 2006, 'Everyone knows that if there is no Doha Agreement, we are perfectly capable of moving ahead on the bilateral track.'[3]

While bilateral initiatives have generally resulted in only limited expansion of intra-PTA trade, suggesting the continued importance of multilateral initiatives, the shift towards bilateral agreements has accelerated over time. The Obama administration in the US has pursued both a Transatlantic Trade and Investment Partnership (TTIP) with the European Union and a Trans-Pacific Partnership (TPP) with countries in the Asia-Pacific region, while significantly diminishing US investment in rescuing the Doha Round. Developing countries have also found bilateral agreements increasingly appealing, especially because south–south agreements may be entered into via the GATT Enabling Clause, whose requirements are far less stringent than the restrictions imposed by Article XXIV on north–north and north–south agreements. This is an unhealthy trend that greatly risks undermining the global trading system.

The successes of multilateral trade liberalisation

World trade in goods and services is much freer today than in the pre-WTO era. Tariff barriers and non-tariff barriers have been significantly reduced, with tariff protection against industrial products at a historic low in almost all countries.[4] Trade outcomes have mirrored this liberalisation, with trade in both goods and services expanding at an accelerated pace. The simple average of annual growth rates of world merchandise exports rose from 5.6% during 1981–94 to 8.9% during 1995–2010.[5] Trade has grown faster than GDP, which grew at an annual global average of 2.2% during both aforementioned periods. Furthermore, merchandise exports have shown remarkable growth in three major regions of the world: Europe, North America and Asia. Though exports are much smaller, export growth in three other regions – Africa, the Middle East and the Commonwealth of Independent States[6] – has been as impressive as in Asia.

Growth in the exports of commercial services has been similarly spectacular. In North America they almost doubled, in Europe they more than doubled, and in Asia they more than tripled between 2000 and 2010. The remaining three regions also saw their commercial-services exports nearly, or more than, triple. Thus, the WTO has been a huge success in facilitating trade.

A key function of the WTO is to implement existing agreements among member countries, and when it replaced GATT it brought in a binding dispute-settlement system backing a damaged party's right to retaliate in the case of an offending party's non-compliance. International trade law expert William J. Davey, who has studied WTO dispute-settlement procedures in detail, concludes that despite some shortcomings the system has lived up to expectations.[7]

It is noteworthy that despite the global financial crisis of 2008, which created high levels of unemployment in the major industrial economies that continue today, trade disruption has been minimal. This is in contrast to the Great Depression when similar dislocations led to a virtual trade war between Europe and the US, which escalated with Washington's enactment of the infamous Smoot–Hawley Tariff in 1930.[8] On the whole, trade has recovered relatively quickly in the aftermath of the 2008 crisis.

Developing countries move towards liberalisation

The last two decades have also seen a serious shift in the attitudes and policies of developing countries towards international trade. In the 1950s and 1960s, development thinking was dominated by the view that developing countries needed to foster industrialisation, and that this required the protection of manufacturing against competition from well-established foreign suppliers. By the late 1980s, however, three factors led to a change in ethos in favour of trade liberalisation in developing countries: the outstanding economic performance of the few developing countries that switched to a liberal trade regime early on, such as South Korea and Taiwan; the failure of protection to produce industrialisation; and the aggressive push towards liberal trade by the World Bank and IMF under loan conditionality. Although initially resented, this last factor eventually contributed to the shift in attitudes.

The outcomes have been impressive. Spurred by trade liberalisation and other market-friendly reforms, China and India both experienced double-digit growth in their exports averaging around 15% annually between 1990 and 2010. Middle-income economies such as Brazil, Indonesia, South Korea, Thailand and Turkey increased their exports nearly 10% annually. Overall, low- and middle-income countries more than doubled their share of global trade, from roughly 20% in 1990 to more than 40% in 2010. With the increased importance of the south in overall world trade, south–south trade flows also increased substantially.[9] Specifically, the share of exports from low-income countries going to low- and middle-income markets has nearly doubled from 22% to over 40% of the total; and the share of exports from middle-income countries to low- and middle-income markets has increased from around 30% to nearly 50%. Furthermore, those countries' overall trade shares have grown much faster than their output.

While special and differential treatment for developing countries continues at the WTO, developing countries today participate much more effectively in the activities of the WTO. This is observed in three principal ways.

Firstly, more developing countries have become members. More than 30 countries have joined the system since the WTO was formed and more than 20 others are negotiating accession. Several interrelated factors have encouraged this. Developing countries have become major exporters of manufactured goods and have thus favoured an outward orientation. The expanded mandate of the WTO has spurred additional participation by developing countries. It covers new areas, such as services, standards and intellectual property rights.

Secondly, developing countries have been far more substantially engaged in the Doha Round than in past multilateral trade negotiations. To begin with, the Doha Round – or Doha 'Development' Agenda as those in the developing world prefer to call it – has focused significant attention on agriculture, a sector vital to developing countries where they would wish to effectively represent their interests in proceedings. The emergence of the G20 grouping prior to the 2003 WTO Ministerial Conference in Mexico and its success in getting the developed countries to drop three of the four 'Singapore issues'[10] from the Doha negotiating agenda, offers one example of their involvement in the negotiating process. Their continued involvement at the Hong Kong Ministerial Conference in 2005, and in the 2008 negotiations in Geneva that produced a deadlock between developed and developing countries, offers another example of the intensity and relevance of their engagement.

Thirdly, developing countries have come to use the WTO Dispute Settlement Body (DSB) to assert and defend their trading rights. Bernard Hoekman[11] points out that while developing countries were defendants in only 8% of GATT cases, they have been defendants in 35% of the cases under the WTO. Developing countries have also emerged as complainants, accounting for one-third of all cases brought to dispute settlement between 1995 and 2011. Just as interestingly, as many as 44% of developing-country suits have been against other developing countries.

Although nearly all developing countries have moved away from the anti-trade policies of the 1950s and 1960s, there are vast differences among them in their trade interests and in their approaches to trade policy. At one extreme are the LDCs that still insist on, and enjoy, overwhelming one-way trade preferences without offering reciprocal liberalisation. These have tariff-free access to the internal EU market under the 'everything but arms' (EBA) initiative. Developing countries in sub-Saharan Africa, the vast majority of them also LDCs, enjoy significant one-way preferences in the US market under the African Growth and Opportunity Act (AGOA). At the other extreme, larger developing countries such as China, Brazil, India and Indonesia have vocally demanded concessions in negotiations. Developing countries in the Cairns Group[12] of primary producers, including Brazil, Argentina, Indonesia and Colombia, played an important role in bringing agriculture into multilateral trade negotiations even during the 1986–94 Uruguay Round.

This emergence of developing countries as significant players in the world trade system, and the heterogeneity of interests among them, has had its own impact on the multilateral process.

The proliferation of preferential agreements

A cornerstone of the WTO is the principle of non-discrimination: member countries may not discriminate against goods entering their borders based on their country of origin. However, in an important exception, through Article XXIV of GATT and Article V of the General Agreement on Trade in Services (GATS), the WTO does permit countries to enter into PTAs with one another in the form of free-trade areas and customs unions. Additional derogation of the principle of non-discrimination is found in the Enabling Clause, which allows one-way tariff preferences to be granted by developed to developing countries, and permits PTAs among developing countries that are not subject to the disciplines imposed by GATT Article XXIV.[13]

Such preferential agreements are now in vogue, with hundreds of them having been negotiated during the last two decades and every member country belonging to several. Ever since they began gathering momentum, PTAs have been called an unfortunate development and a threat to multilateral liberalisation.[14] The proponents of bilateral agreements, on the other hand, have argued that PTAs are designed to complement rather than supplant multilateral liberalisation and that bilateral approaches may yield faster liberalisation than that achieved through multilateral negotiation. They thus defend a 'WTO-plus' approach to trade liberalisation.

The actual record on trade liberalisation through bilateral negotiations paints a different picture, however, and the analysis provided by the recent *World Trade Report (WTR) 2011* is instructive in this regard.[15] The *WTR 2011* reports that there has been a significant increase in the value of trade taking place between PTA members. In 1990, trade between PTA partners (excluding intra-EU trade) made up around 18% of world trade and this figure rose to 35% by 2008. However, only about 16% of world trade actually enjoys a preference (when we exclude intra-EU trade) and only 30% when we include it. Furthermore, less than 2% of trade (4% when intra-EU trade is included) takes place in goods that receive a tariff preference greater than 10%. This is because the majority of the trade under most PTAs takes place under Most Favoured Nation (MFN) tariffs set at zero. Only a small fraction of trade between PTA members is conducted on a preferential basis, especially outside the EU and the North American Free Trade Agreement (NAFTA) between the US, Canada and Mexico.[16]

It is also now clear that PTAs have become a stumbling block to multilateral liberalisation. Exporters, especially in developed countries, have learned that they get better deals through PTAs, since they gain an upper hand over non-members. They therefore prefer the bilateral, rather than the multilateral, route to liberalisation. This is also often true of firms with multinational investments. Some argue that the multilateral process has suffered because large US firms have increasingly become multinational, with investments in multiple foreign countries reducing their incentive to seek liberalisation in those countries through the USTR, because that would open them up to competition in those foreign markets from firms from other parts of the world. These US multinationals have lost credibility with the USTR, which no longer sees them as necessarily pushing purely US interests; and this has weakened a major lobby within the US that favoured multilateral liberalisation. This has been less of an impediment to preferential liberalisation, as this only extends to firms in the home country and, further, specific sectors may be chosen for liberalisation and others excluded.

PTAs may impede multilateral liberalisation even further in the context of developed-country lobbies pushing non-trade agenda items such as intellectual property rights and labour standards. Large developing countries such as India, China and Brazil are strictly opposed to the further proliferation of non-trade issues within the WTO. That naturally diverts such lobbies towards PTAs, where they face much weaker developing-country partners and have relatively free rein. The US in particular is playing the game almost entirely as predicted[17] – a hegemonic power is likely to gain a greater pay-off by bargaining sequentially with a group of non-hegemonic powers rather than simultaneously.

Avoiding multilateral negotiations also allows countries to maintain distortions in agriculture. As an example, US cotton subsidies can continue indefinitely so long as they remain outside the multilateral negotiation process. Buyers of subsidised US cotton, such as Bangladesh, profit from its lower price when exporting apparel they have manufactured from it. Meanwhile, other cotton exporters from West Africa and India cannot challenge the subsidies in the WTO.

We should also discuss the link between forums for trade negotiation and the evolving phenomena of production fragmentation and trade, aka global value chains. Production fragmentation describes the situation in which various components of a good are produced in multiple countries and possibly traverse national borders many times before being assembled into the final form sold to the consumer.[18] Some now claim that the fragmentation of global production provides a new basis for countries to achieve preferential integration regionally, and at a 'deeper' level. Yet, it would seem that production fragmentation should instead provide greater incentives for broader multilateral liberalisation.[19] After all, the most efficient producers of any given intermediate good need not lie within the jurisdictional boundaries of any specific preferential agreement, and the identity and location of the most efficient producers of intermediates may be expected to vary faster than any country's ability to sign new preferential agreements. With increased fragmentation, the identification of the origin of goods, so that preferences may be suitably granted, is another major challenge. If PTAs were designed to support fragmented production networks, we might expect to see greater geographic concentration of trade over time as many production networks are regional in nature. However, as the *WTR 2011* notes, the share of intra-regional trade in Europe remained roughly constant from 1990 to 2009, at around 73%. While Asia's intra-regional trade seems to have risen from 42% to 52% during the same period, North America's intra-regional trade shares rose from 41% in 1990 to 56% in 2000, before falling back to 48% in 2009.[20] Therefore, it cannot be argued that preferential agreements have been designed to support or benefit from fragmented production networks. The multiple crossings of borders by a single good before it takes its final form only makes the WTO more relevant; in this case, knocking down tariffs multilaterally, or otherwise facilitating trade, as negotiated recently at the multilateral level in Bali, has even greater value.

The Doha Round

The multilateral Doha Round was one of three major trade agreements being negotiated at the start of 2015; the other two were major preferential deals pursued by the US: the TPP and the TTIP. Sometimes called the Doha Development Agenda because of its putative focus on the improvement of developing countries' trading prospects, this multilateral round was launched in 2001. The Doha ministerial declaration mandated the round to negotiate liberalisation in agriculture, services and intellectual property rights. Despite several attempts to advance the negotiations, it still has not been successfully closed, although preliminary agreement on less contentious issues such as trade facilitation and the removal of trade barriers against exports from LDCs was finally achieved at the December 2013 WTO Ministerial Conference in Bali. Until this admittedly minor breakthrough, many observers thought the round had reached an impasse, with some going so far as to suggest that it should now be officially killed off.

Why have the Doha negotiations stalled? Several explanations account for the situation. Because the Doha discussions have lasted well over a decade, with changing domestic and global economic environments and changing negotiating details, individual countries' wishes have varied over time.

Developing countries' expectations of the so-called 'development' round were at least partly based on the idea that the previous Uruguay Round of negotiations had effectively damaged them and that the new round would be about treating those injuries. This impression was greatly reinforced by repeated assertions by the heads of international institutions, journalists, NGOs and many influential academics that agricultural protection was largely a developed-country problem. Developed-country subsidies and protection, this argument ran, hurt the poorest developing countries the most; it was wrong to ask the poor countries to liberalise when rich countries heavily protected their own markets; and agricultural subsidies and protection in the rich countries was a case of double standards and hypocrisy on the part of rich countries. The effect of these assertions was to considerably harden the stance of the developing countries and to give them false hope that they would be granted one-way concessions from developed countries, especially in agriculture.

The initial goal of many food-exporting developing countries was the reduction of developed-country production and export subsidies – so that the price of these developed countries' food exports would rise. However, the 2007–08 food-price crisis, when shortages of particular commodities led to sharp increases in food prices, led them to re-evaluate this position. Indeed, many developing countries are now more interested in keeping food prices in check than in eliminating developed-country subsidies.

Equally, some countries have been fearful of the opposite outcome, whereby imports might push agricultural prices too far down. For instance, in 2008, there was resolute disagreement between India and China, on the one hand, and the US, on the other, over the special safeguard mechanism, a measure ostensibly designed to protect poor farmers by allowing countries to impose a special tariff on certain agricultural goods in the event of an import surge. Thus, countries have shown a degree of ambivalence towards a rationalisation of agricultural policy, and perhaps see this as less of a priority than previously.

Even without agreement at Doha, agricultural export subsidies have nearly disappeared and actionable domestic agricultural subsidies have come down considerably in both the EU and US.

In the US, actionable domestic subsidies have similarly declined. As a result of reforms to the EU's Common Agricultural Policy, support for beef, olive oil, fruits and vegetables, as measured by the current total Aggregate Measure of Support (AMS),[21] has either declined sharply or ceased altogether. Support for cereals, dairy and sugar remains more significant, but overall support has considerably declined. Between 2000/01 and 2007/08, Amber Box subsidies (i.e., those which WTO agreements recommend be reduced) in the EU had dropped to 12.4 billion euros. Similarly, in the US, the total support in 2007 fell to US$84.65bn, of which US$76.2bn was under the Green Box (permitted subsidies) category. Total AMS was down to US$6.3bn.

Finally, in seeking to understand why the Doha Round has stalled, it is important to note that the heft of emerging economies has increased dramatically in recent years. A much greater fraction of the growth in world GDP came from developing countries in the last decade than it did in the preceding decade. So rich countries are much more concerned about access to emerging markets than they were when the goals for the Doha Round were first set. Indeed, the US sees the Doha talks as an important opportunity to get fast-growing emerging economies to reduce their duties on imports of manufactured goods, which were reduced in previous rounds but remain higher than those in developed countries.

Interestingly, markets in industrial goods and services in developing countries also underwent significant liberalisation in the 2000s. This was particularly true of two major countries: China and India. As a part of the conditions for its 2001 entry into the WTO, China undertook major obligations to liberalise. It not only undertook this liberalisation de facto, but also made it binding at the WTO, giving it international legal force. India continued to bring its tariffs down and open service sectors to direct foreign investment until at least 2007–08 as a part of its national liberalisation. Outside of agriculture, which remains highly protected, it now has a very open trade regime, with the trade in goods and services rising to above 50% of GDP. These developments have perhaps left some of the major developing-country players more or less satisfied in terms of market access, especially as they seem to lack the appetite to further open their own markets to the extent necessary to bring the Doha Round to a conclusion.

The Trans-Pacific Partnership (TPP)

The TPP is a trade agreement under negotiation between the US and 11 other countries: Australia, Brunei, Canada, Chile, Japan, Malaysia, Mexico, New Zealand, Peru, Singapore and Vietnam. It is sometimes seen as a competitor to the Regional Comprehensive Economic Partnership (RCEP) being championed by China and discussed by ASEAN's ten member states, along with Australia, China, Japan, India, South Korea and New Zealand. The US, which has led the TPP negotiations, sees the agreement as providing a link to the dynamic economies of the Asia-Pacific and insurance against its exclusion from the RCEP.

While the TPP covers many standard items, such as the liberalisation of trade in goods and services, several of its provisions have been criticised as excessively restrictive. For instance, the provisions relating to intellectual property protection – the enforcement of patents and copyrights – provide restraints well beyond those in previous bilateral trade agreements negotiated by the US, let alone those in the WTO Trade-Related Aspects of Intellectual Property Rights (TRIPS) Agreement. In particular, concerns have been expressed that the TPP focuses on protecting intellectual property to the detriment of efforts to provide affordable medicine in the developing world, thus going against the foreign-policy goals of the Obama administration.

In addition, there have been strong domestic pressures within the US for the inclusion of a 'labour chapter' that, for instance, ensures that workers in any TPP country have the ability to unionise and engage in collective wage bargaining. This may seem hypocritical since an astonishingly small proportion of the US labour force is unionised today.

The TPP is widely discussed and considered as a prelude to far broader economic integration across the Asia-Pacific. Proponents argue that it could establish an 'open regionalism' framework for other countries to sign on without being subject to the exhausting negotiations required for bilateral agreements. Specifically, countries could simply elect to join the TPP via what has been called a 'docking' arrangement. It has been suggested that the Trans-Pacific Partnership could be the last trade agreement that the US negotiates and henceforth other countries could simply elect to join the TPP. However, given the provisions relating to intellectual property rights protection and the labour-standards clauses, it is unlikely that two of the largest countries in Asia, China and India, will join the TPP. As Jagdish Bhagwati has noted, if accepting these remains a precondition for joining the TPP, the result may be a fragmentation of Asia into three spheres: TPP, China and India. [22]

Transatlantic Trade and Investment Partnership (TTIP)

The US is also negotiating a TTIP with the European Union, but this has already missed its first deadline for completion at the end of 2014, thanks to current economic circumstances and long-standing differences between the two parties.

Economic circumstances in several EU countries remain dire, as the eurozone has failed to recover from the banking and financial crisis of recent years. Unemployment stands at around 12% overall and is significantly higher in the hardest-hit countries such as Greece, where unemployment is nearly 30% and youth unemployment higher still at nearly 65%. Under these circumstances, it seems highly unlikely that an ambitious trade programme with potentially major distributional consequences will find support among the 28 different EU states.

Moreover, while tariff barriers between the US and the EU are already quite low, the negotiations are likely to be plagued by differences on economic and regulatory matters. Decades-long differences of perspective and priorities exist in areas such as agricultural subsidy and protection, health and safety, cultural diversity and protection, competition policy, services regulation, genetically modified (GM) foods and environmental regulations. It is extremely unlikely that the persistent differences in viewpoints, supported by popular sentiment, entrenched interest groups and domestic regulators, will be ironed out – despite the priority evidently given to the proposed agreement by the top political leadership. Indeed, powerful political actors on both sides have already taken tough negotiating positions, insisting on their favoured regulatory templates, such as on GM foods and environmental standards, while insisting that any attempts to pursue an agreement with more limited goals would be doomed to failure.

Bilateral versus multilateral rule-making and dispute settlement

Doha Round negotiations cover a variety of issues and sectors such as agriculture, services, investment and intellectual property, all now comprehensively negotiated within the WTO realm. In addition to discussions about market access, much needs to be done in these and other areas in terms of rule-making. For instance, rules governing trade in services require negotiation over complex issues in areas such as competition policy, domestic regulation and government procurement.

While past rule-making has largely occurred during multi-lateral negotiation rounds, it is unclear how this will evolve in future. The question is whether the weakening of the multi-lateral trade process and the popularity of bilateral processes might damage the rule-making function of the WTO and result in a clashing set of rules specific to separate bilateral agreements.

The problem is an especially acute one for developing countries; the intense regulation of services trade and the complexity of the consultative processes at all levels – plus a lack of information on institutional best practices and the commercial interests of individual countries – has made them cautious and defensive about rule-making in multilateral forums. But the more progress on these rule-making lags at the multilateral level, the greater the risk that developing-country markets will be harvested individually by dominant trading partners who offer bilateral agreements setting the rules to reflect their own interests.

A similar issue arises with respect to the dispute-settlement mechanism. This would also be undermined if the WTO were to be perceived as weakened or merely optional, and disputes were resolved in other bilateral and regional forums instead. Many of the preferential trade agreements negotiated since the WTO came into existence cover areas already subject to obligations under WTO agreements – for instance on intellectual property, services, government procurement and technical barriers to trade. These PTAs typically contain provisions on dispute settlement that establish committees and detail procedures for handling disputes between the parties to the agreement; and this is potentially problematic, because these procedures and committees need not coincide with those at the WTO. As legal academic Peter Drahos has noted, a distinctive feature of the PTAs signed by the US is that the dispute-settlement chapters give the complainant state a 'choice of forum' in those cases where 'the state complained against has breached an obligation under more than one trade agreement and both states are parties to the relevant trade agreements'. The ability of a dominant state to choose its legal battleground clearly has implications for weaker states. This would be especially true if the stronger state were to choose to pursue the case in a setting other than that of the WTO DSB. As Drahos concludes, 'Weaker states are probably making themselves worse off by agreeing to such provisions.'[23]

Failure of the Doha Round will effectively lead the WTO DSB to write the rules itself rather than to just interpret them. When WTO ministers, who act as the organisation's 'legislature', fail to clarify the rules and cases come to the DSB, judgments will have to be delivered even where extant rules are ambiguous. Once these judgments are given, however, new rules will effectively be created through precedent. Thus, it remains essential that multilateral negotiations succeed in the rule-making sphere.[24]

Conclusion

The global trading system remains open and world trade has seen healthy growth since the inception of the WTO. Remarkably, the Lehman crisis did no lasting damage to the institution and, after a brief setback, global trade recovered remarkably rapidly. This being said, there remains a threat to the WTO as long as the Doha Round of multilateral negotiations is not satisfactorily closed. Despite recent success in Bali and suggested innovations to move the negotiations forward, such as 'mini-ministerial' meetings, failure to achieve the main goals of the Doha Round remains a distinct possibility. This would leave preferential trade agreements as the only game in town, which would undermine not only the trade-liberalisation function of the WTO, but also its rule-making role. In this context, the United States' recent focus on two major PTAs – the TPP and TTIP – is worrisome. As it stands, the prospects for a successful negotiation of the TTIP look dim and the successful closure of even the TPP faces numerous uphill tasks. However, if these arrangements become reality, they would greatly diminish US interest in the WTO, which would relegate the institution to a secondary role.

Notes

1   The Havana Charter creating the ITO was signed in March 1948 but it was never ratified by the US Congress, leaving international trade to be managed via GATT.

2   While the textile sector was significantly liberalised in the Uruguay Round, both agriculture and services remain subject to enormous distortions and thus offer the potential for significant economic gains, if suitably liberalised. This is a fact that appears to have been overlooked by recent commentators expressing the concern that multilateral liberalisation has little to offer, as much of the liberalisation has already been undertaken in preceding multilateral negotiation rounds.

3   Quoted in Alan Beattie and Edward Alden, 'US not prepared to accept '"Doha lite"', *Financial Times*, 10 June 2006.

4   For details on trade liberalisation beyond that contained in this chapter, see Arvind Panagariya, 'The Free Trade Area of the Americas: Good for Latin America?', *World Economy*, vol. 19, no. 5, September 1996, pp. 485–515.

5   These rates have been calculated using the annual growth rates in Appendix table A1 in *International Trade Statistics 2011* (Geneva: World Trade Organisation, 2011).

6   Russia and the former Soviet Republics of Armenia, Azerbaijan, Belarus, Kazakhstan, Kyrgyzstan, Moldova, Tajikistan and Uzbekistan.

7   William Davey, 'The future of the WTO: what is next for the WTO?', Paper presented at Stanford University Conference on the

Future of the WTO, Stanford Center for International Development, 26–27 April 2012.

8 The Tariff Act of 1930, commonly referred to as the Smoot–Hawley Tariff, significantly raised US tariffs on nearly 900 products. Other countries retaliated and world trade contracted sharply – by 66% between 1929 and 1934.

9 Further details on these patterns of south–south trade can be found in Pravin Krishna and Matthias Matthijs, 'Trading Up or Trading Down: Emerging Markets' Changing Interests in the World Trade System', *SAISPHERE* (the magazine of Johns Hopkins School of Advanced International Studies), 2013–14, pp. 28–31.

10 These so-called 'Singapore issues' are: transparency in government procurement; trade facilitation (customs issues); trade and investment; and trade and competition. Only work on trade facilitation continues.

11 See Bernard Hoekman, 'Emerging Economies and the WTO', Paper presented at Stanford University Conference on the Future of the WTO, Stanford Center for International Development, 26–27 April 2012.

12 The Cairns Group of agricultural exporters was formed in 1986 to lobby at the Uruguay Round for the liberalisation of trade in agricultural products. Taking the name of the Australian town where the first meeting was held, the initiative was spearheaded by producers in both developed and developing countries who wished to make sure that their products were not locked out of markets in Europe and Asia.

13 Article XXIV of the General Agreement on Tariffs and Trade (GATT) 1994, http://www.wto.org/english/docs_e/legal_e/gatt47_02_e.htm#articleXXIV.

14 The earliest systematic critique of preferential trade agreements was provided by Jadish Bhagwati in 'Regionalism and Multilateralism: An Overview', in Jaime de Melo and Arvind Panagariya (eds), *New Dimensions in Regional Integration* (Cambridge: Cambridge University Press, 2007). Subsequent contributions in this spirit include Jagdish Bhagwati and Arvind Panagariya, 'Preferential Trading Areas and Multilateralism: Strangers, Friends or Foes?', in Bhagwati and Panagariya (eds), *The Economics of Preferential Trading* (Washington DC: AEI Press, pp. 1–78); Panagariya, 'The Regionalism Debate: An Overview', *World Economy*, vol. 22, no. 4, 1999, pp. 455–76; and Pravin Krishna, 'Preferential Trade Agreements and the World Trade System: A Multilateralist View', in Robert Feenstra and Alan Taylor (eds), *Globalization in an Age of Crisis: Multilateral Cooperation in the Twenty-First Century* (Chicago, Il: University of Chicago Press, 2013). An accessible survey of the theory of preferential trading is provided by Panagariya, 'Preferential Trade Liberalisation: The Traditional Theory and New Developments', *Journal of Economic Literature,* vol. 38, no. 3, June 2000, pp. 477–511.

15 *World Trade Report 2011 – The WTO and preferential trade agreements: From co-existence to coherence* (Geneva: World Trade Organisation, 2011).

[16] Ironically, it is conceivable that the difficulty with complying with the rules of origin within preferential agreements is large enough to at least partially explain the low take-up of PTA preferences by firms, especially small and medium-sized enterprises. For a detailed discussion, see the *World Trade Report 2011*.

[17] See, for example, Jagdish Bhagwati, 'Threats to the World Trading System: Income Distribution and the Selfish Hegemon', *Journal of International Affairs*, vol. 48, Spring 1994, pp. 279–85.

[18] The fragmentation of trade and its increased relevance over time has been well documented in the economics literature. For instance, Varian points out that the iPod music player is made from more than 400 parts that originate in several different countries and are finally assembled in China; see Hal Varian, 'An iPod Has Global Value, Ask the (Many) Countries That Make It', *New York Times*, 28 June 2007.

[19] Indeed, at a more basic level, the various theoretical aspects of production networks, such as trade in intermediates, foreign investment and multinational production and so on, are old issues in the literature and do not interfere with the basic welfare propositions concerning the dominance of multilateral free trade over other policies.

[20] The principal factor behind the rise in intra-regional trade in Asia is the liberalisation and faster growth in the countries within this region. This also explains in large part the decline in intra-regional trade in North America during the 2000s, despite NAFTA, which has worked to divert trade towards regional partners.

[21] Aggregate Measurement of Support (AMS) means the annual level of support, expressed in monetary terms, provided for an agricultural product in favour of the producers of the basic agricultural product or non-product-specific support provided in favour of agricultural producers in general, excluding support provided under programmes that qualify as exempt from reduction under Annex 2 to the Uruguay Round Agreement on Agriculture.

[22] Bhagwati, 'Threats to the World trading System'.

[23] Peter Drahos, 'Weaving Webs of Influence: The United States, Free Trade Agreements and Dispute Resolution', *Journal of World Trade*, vol. 41, no. 1, 2007, pp. 191–210.

[24] As an example, experts are sharply divided on whether the current WTO rules allow a carbon tax on imports. Under these circumstances, if a country such as the US were to introduce a carbon tax on imports and it were challenged in the WTO, the Dispute Settlement Body would have to take a view on the matter even though the existing rules do not provide clear guidance one way or the other.

CHAPTER TWO

Ideas and power in contemporary trade development

Arvind Subramanian

The future of global trade and trade policy is likely to be shaped by two important developments – namely, the challenge of globalisation in the West, especially the United States; and impending mega-regionalism, involving the largest trading economies in the world: the US, Europe, Japan and possibly China. The challenge of the West illustrates a struggle between the objectives of globalisation and broader forces – including economic stagnation and inequality – that may undermine the ability to sustain globalisation. The initiation of mega-regionalism by the US is really an opening shot in a much bigger game between a stagnant or declining power (the US) and a rising power facing its own challenges (China).

Features of recent globalisation

In my 2014 article with Martin Kessler, we identified seven major features of the current era of trade integration and of today's trading system.[1] Of these, three are particularly relevant to the future of the global trading system: the 'hyper-globalisation' of trade; the rise of the first mega-trader (China) since Imperial Britain; and the proliferation of regional trade agreements and the approach of mega-regional deals.[2]

Hyper-globalisation

Since the 1990s, aided by broad-based rapid growth ('convergence with a vengeance'), the world entered a fourth phase of trade integration that we dubbed 'hyper-globalisation'. World trade has soared much more rapidly than world GDP. Merchandise exports-to-GDP ratios soared from 15% to 26%, and goods and services exports to about 33%, over the course of the past two decades. This rapid increase is somewhat surprising, because transport costs do not appear to have declined as rapidly as in earlier eras.[3]

However, the cost of information and communications did decline significantly.

Part of the increase in trade reflects the fragmentation of manufacturing across borders – the famous slicing up of the value-added chain as individual production stages are located where the costs of production are lowest. This phenomenon, whereby technology no longer requires that successive stages of manufacturing production be physically contiguous or proximate, has been dubbed the 'second unbundling'.[4]

The years between 1870 and 1914 have been described as the first golden age of globalisation. World trade as a share of gross domestic product (GDP) surged from 9% in 1870 to 16% on the eve of the First World War. This was the era about which John Maynard Keynes waxed eloquently, noting that an inhabitant of London 'could order by telephone, sipping his morning tea in bed, the various products of the whole earth, in such quantity as he might see fit, and reasonably expect their early delivery upon his doorstep'.[5]

The period between 1914 and the end of the Second World War witnessed the 'Great Reversal' of globalisation, as a

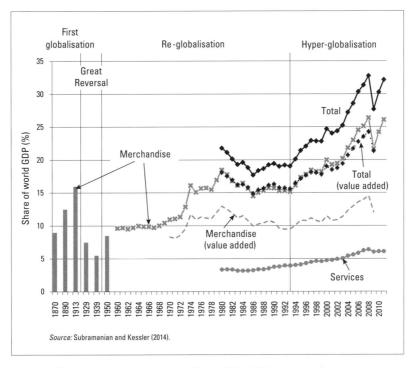

Figure 1. **World exports, in current dollars, 1870–2011**

combustible mix of isolationism, nationalism and militarism ignited protectionist policies. World trade plunged to 5.5% of world GDP just before the Second World War began.[6]

A third era, starting after the Second World War, saw the restoration of world trade, aided by declines in transport costs and trade barriers. Only by about the mid- to late 1970s did world trade revert to the peaks seen before the First World War.

Two related features of this era of hyper-globalisation are the rise of multinational corporations and the sharp surge in foreign direct investment (FDI), which have both caused and been caused by cross-border and other flows of goods and services. Since the early 1990s, broadly coinciding with the era of hyper-globalisation, FDI flows have outpaced GDP growth. Global FDI as a share of world GDP, which hovered around 0.5%, increased sevenfold, peaking at close to 4% just before the onset of the 2008 global financial crisis.[7]

China's rise as a mega-trader

A mega-trader can be defined in two senses: globally (relative to world trade) and nationally (relative to a country's own output). On the first criterion, Japan was a mega-trader in the 1980s, accounting for about 7.5% of global trade at its peak.[8] Based on this criterion, none of the other East Asian tiger economies would have been noteworthy, despite their astonishing performance; the small economies of Singapore, Hong Kong (China), Taiwan (China) and Malaysia accounted for a very small share of world trade at their peaks. Since 1990, however, a true mega-trader has emerged: China. It qualifies as such under both definitions of the term. Its integration into the world trade system accelerated with its accession to the WTO in 2001, and transformed the country into the world's largest exporter (and importer of manufactured goods, having surpassed the United States in 2012; *see Table 1*).

China's exports and imports are more than 50% of GDP.[9] When its size and income level are taken into account, it is a substantial over-trader, comparable to the United Kingdom in the heyday of empire and a vastly bigger trader than the

Table 1. **Merchandise exports as percentage of world exports by mega-traders, 1870–2030**

Year	United Kingdom	Germany	United States	Japan	China
1870	24.3	13.4	5.0	0.1	2.8
1913	18.5	18.0	9.0	0.8	2.0
1929	15.1	16.6	14.4	2.1	3.0
1950	10.2	3.9	16.2	1.3	0.9
1973	5.1	12.9	12.2	6.4	1.0
1990	5.3	12.0	11.3	8.2	1.8
2000	4.4	8.5	12.1	7.4	3.9
2012	2.6	7.7	8.4	4.4	11.2
2020 (projected)	1.9	5.3	8.8	3.9	12.1
2030 (projected)	1.4	3.6	7.3	3.2	15.0

Sources: Angus Maddison, *Monitoring the World Economy, 1820–1995* (Paris: OECD, 1995); UN Conference on Trade and Development (UNCTAD), various years; Arvind Subramanian, *Eclipse: Living in the Shadow of China's Economic Dominance* (Washington DC: Peterson Institute for International Economics, 2011); and authors' projections.

United States, Japan or Germany at their peaks. In fact, China is the first mega-trader since Imperial Britain. If trade continues to grow in line with income, China's dominance in world trade will become even greater.

Preferential trade and growing regionalisation

The era of hyper-globalisation has been accompanied by a proliferation of preferential trade agreements (PTAs, *see Figure 2*). Today, about half of the exports of the top 30 exporters go to preferential trade partners. Between 1990 and 2010, the number of PTAs increased from 70 to 300. In the mid-1990s, about 75% of PTAs were regional; by 2003, this share had dropped to about 50%. All World Trade Organisation (WTO) members except Mongolia have concluded at least one PTA; the EU, Chile and Mexico have concluded more than 20.

An interesting new dimension of these PTAs is the extent to which they feature 'deep integration',[10] liberalising not only

Figure 2. **New preferential trade agreements, 1958–2012**

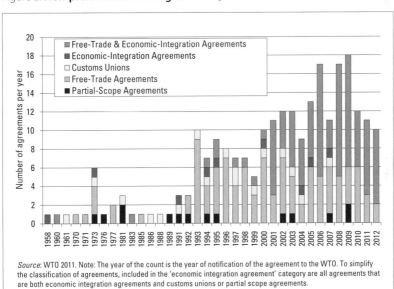

Source: WTO 2011. Note: The year of the count is the year of notification of the agreement to the WTO. To simplify the classification of agreements, included in the 'economic integration agreement' category are all agreements that are both economic integration agreements and customs unions or partial scope agreements.

tariffs and quotas but 'behind-the-border' barriers, such as regulations and standards, too. In the last ten years, for example, nearly 40 agreements have included provisions on WTO-plus issues, such as competition policy, intellectual property rights, investment and the movement of capital.

On regional agreements, seismic changes are under way, with the negotiation of possible mega-regional agreements between the United States and Asia (the Trans-Pacific Partnership, TPP) and the US and EU (the Transatlantic Trade and Investment Partnership, TTIP). Trade between these groups of countries accounts for some US$2 trillion to US$3 trn a year, signifying a potentially major jump in the volume of world trade covered by preferential agreements. These PTAs would represent the first between the top four global regions (China, the US, Europe and Japan), with important consequences.

The West's challenge

The Pew Research Center found in 2010 that US public support for free-trade agreements was at its lowest point since 2006 – and the decline occurred quickly. In 2009, the share of people who supported free-trade agreements exceeded the share who opposed them by a margin of 11 percentage points. In 2010, opponents of free trade outnumbered supporters by eight percentage points.[11]

Surprisingly, the turnaround was even more dramatic among Republican-leaning voters: the margin in 2009 was seven percentage points in favour of free-trade agreements; the margin in 2010 was 26 percentage points against free-trade agreements. This weakening collective perception of the benefits of openness is matched, mirrored, or validated by intellectual opinion.[12]

That several leading intellectuals – instinctively cosmopolitan and ideologically liberal – talk like this is an important signal, not least because the objective circumstances have changed. One might call this challenge that of the irresistible force of globalisation and hyper-globalisation meeting the immovable object of weakening economic and fiscal fortunes in the West.

In the US, except for a brief spell in the late 1990s, median wages have stagnated for three decades; inequality has been sharply rising, particularly because of rising incomes at the very top of the income spectrum;[13] and mobility has declined.[14] As in all industrial countries, indebtedness has risen, with average debt in the G7 now about 80% of GDP. Prospects for medium-term growth are not bright, according to the 2014 *World Economic Outlook*,[15] while ageing and other entitlements add to the serious fiscal pressures ahead. These are not the most propitious conditions for sustaining globalisation.

The policy challenge in the advanced countries is that sustaining current levels of openness will involve addressing these domestic challenges exactly when growth could be slowing and the ability to effect redistribution is being impeded by broader medium-term fiscal concerns. Changing Western attitudes to globalisation and free trade are unsurprising, given this.

Dani Rodrik[16] has argued that sustaining openness requires a domestic social consensus behind it, which in turn requires mechanisms of social insurance to cushion domestic actors against globalisation-induced shocks. Rodrik provides evidence that this domestic consensus can be captured in the relationship between the size of government (a proxy for social-insurance mechanisms) and openness.

More direct evidence of the importance of social insurance comes from David Autor, David Dorn and Gordon Hanson,[17] who show that rising exposure to Chinese imports increases unemployment, lowers labour-force participation and reduces wages in local labour markets. Transfer payments for unemployment, disability, retirement and healthcare also rise sharply in exposed labour markets. Autor et al. estimate the increase in annual per capita transfers attributable to rising Chinese import competition at US$32 in the first ten years and US$51 in the last seven years of the sample, which translates into total expenditure of about US$5 billion in the 1990s and almost US$15bn in the 2000s. The dead-weight loss of financing these transfers is one-third to two-thirds as large as US gains from trade with China.

Can the West sustain these social-insurance mechanisms? According to Larry Summers, globalisation both increases the need for social insurance and undermines the government's ability to provide it, because it renders several factors, especially capital and highly skilled labour, more mobile and less easy to tax.[18] Has capital become less easy to tax? Evidence suggests that the marginal effective tax rates on capital in some important member states of the Organisation for Economic Cooperation and Development (OECD), and for the OECD as a whole, have been sharply declining, and there is little pressure to reverse these trends. For the OECD as a whole, the average marginal tax rate declined from about 55% to almost 40%. These declines were witnessed across most, if not all, countries. In the US, rates declined from 65% to just over 50%; in Germany they fell from about 60% to less than 50%. Of course, these declines reflect pressures other than globalisation and the attendant difficulty of heavily taxing mobile capital, but these pressures have been important.

A new development adds to the problems. Across the OECD, the share of the economic pie accruing to capital has been increasing, from about 35% to 40% in the last few years. In his highly acclaimed 2014 book, *Capital in the Twenty-First Century*, Thomas Piketty warned that the tendency of capital to garner even larger shares of the pie is likely to continue.[19] This increasing share has prompted several commentators, including Paul Krugman, to argue that the debate about inequality and trade in the 1990s, which related to inequality between skilled and unskilled labour, should now be viewed through a different lens, because inequality is increasingly between labour and those who own capital.[20]

For the purposes of our argument, what is important is this: not only is the ability to finance mechanisms of social insurance being undermined by weak growth and the burden of debt;[21] slippery, mobile capital is now accounting for a larger share of the economic pie. The funding of social insurance through taxation is thus going to become more difficult.

Protectionism averted

Several commentators have remarked on the fact that despite suffering perhaps the biggest global trade shock in the recent worldwide financial crisis, nations did not succumb to protectionism. This response stood in stark contrast to the experience of the 1930s. Explanations for the difference have included the facts that countries were able to use macroeconomic policy instruments (monetary and exchange rate), which adherence to the gold standard initially prevented in the 1930s;[22] automatic stabilisers were in place, by way of transfers and unemployment benefits;[23] and the deeper integration created by modern production chains rendered protectionism self-defeating.[24]

However, the bigger puzzle is this: how did the West, and the US in particular, adjust to arguably the biggest structural trade shock in its history – namely, rising imports from China – without any serious recourse to protectionism? Why was there less protectionist outrage in the US against China than there was against Mexico in the 1990s or Japan in the 1980s?[25]

The differences cannot be explained by the relative magnitude of the three shocks, as the Chinese shock was orders of

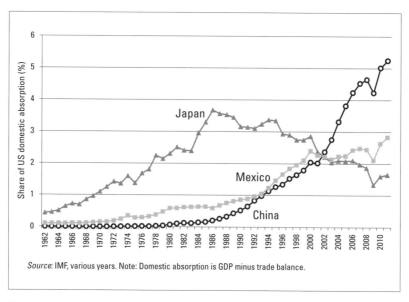

Figure 3. **Import shocks in the US from Mexico, Japan and China, 1962–2011**

magnitude larger than those earlier. Figure 3 plots imports from Mexico, Japan and China as a share of US domestic consumption. At its peak, Japan accounted for 3.6% of US consumption, whereas China accounts for 5.2%.[26] Depending on the measure used, the Chinese shock has been estimated as either four, five or ten times as great as the Japanese and Mexican shocks.[27]

There are several explanations for the differential response to the China shock including whether the China shock is really a measurement issue based on the double counting of exports; whether the US has specialised away from labour-intensive goods;[28] whether China has muted opposition by co-opting US capital by way of FDI; and whether favourable macroeconomic circumstances played a role.

One conclusion from all of this is that if US domestic politics could survive a shock as great as that from China, there may be an underlying resilience – helped considerably by government insurance mechanisms – that should not be underestimated.

Moreover, it could be argued that structural shocks similar to China's are unlikely to repeat themselves. This fact should temper unremitting pessimism about the future of globalisation.

The important question now is whether the idea of globalisation can survive the headwinds of economic forces that are going to keep growth in the US and Europe relatively muted, to strain public balance sheets, to erode the tax base necessary to sustain the political consensus for globalisation, and to cause worsening inequality especially in the US? Should one be sanguine based on the muted response to the China shock or should one be more cautious because of ominous forces threatening globalisation?

Mega-regionalism as a tool to contain China

As previously discussed, Washington has embarked on two major preferential trade initiatives: a Trans-Pacific Partnership (TPP) in the Asia-Pacific; and a Transatlantic Trade and Investment Partnership (TTIP) with the EU.

Why is it doing so? Consider first the TPP. Around 2011, convinced that export dynamism was a key element of reviving growth and shedding the United States' global role as importer and financier of last resort, vulnerable to accusations of business unfriendliness and looking for a bipartisan cause with which to woo Republicans, the Obama administration seized upon trade as a useful policy to pursue.

That decided, free trade with a set of Asian countries held several geostrategic attractions. Firstly, it offered American firms further access to the most economically dynamic region in the world. Secondly, the TPP was more likely to succeed in this form. The TPP model is one of the US, as a large country, negotiating with a set of smaller countries, allowing the US to retain an overwhelming balance of bargaining power. (The inclusion of Japan and Canada in TPP changes that model to some extent but not fundamentally.)

This model matters because the US is increasingly structurally handicapped in trade negotiations that require give and take. By virtue of being a relatively open economy, it does not have much to give. Thus, only with smaller countries is it able to secure opening by others without having to open much itself. From this follows a major TPP feature: broadly asymmetric market opening. The assumption underlying the TPP is that the US would expect partner countries to liberalise their trade and upgrade their regulatory regimes to American standards. The US would undertake some opening – in dairy and textiles, and possibly in diluting export controls – but not a substantial amount. Asymmetric liberalisation would have the political virtue of muting opposition from domestic economic constituencies.

The third geostrategic attraction of the TPP was the opportunity to contain China economically and politically. Especially with Canada, Mexico and Japan brought into the TPP fold, liberalisation within this bloc will raise barriers to Chinese products. In the jargon, there will be trade diversion away from China. Economic containment is embodied in worsening Chinese companies' access to American and Asian markets.

TPP also coincided with, and was a response to, Asian countries' desire for a greater American presence in the region in the wake of Chinese military assertiveness in the East and South China seas. Symbolically, if not substantively, TPP has become emblematic of political containment, in part because Asia wanted it to be so.

The transatlantic deal, the TTIP, will differ from its Pacific counterpart in one crucial respect by requiring broadly symmetric market opening by the US and the EU. The US and Europe are near-equals (or at least not very unequal) in size and power, implying that the US cannot demand of Europe what it will of its TPP partners, namely one-way opening.

The deeper rationales of the TTIP are twofold. It is an attempt to shore up some semblance of Atlantic commonality and community as economic dynamism shifts to Asia. Like the TPP, the TTIP aims to contain China economically, but in a different way. Leveraging the size of two very large markets, the TTIP aims to prevent China from imposing its technical standards – in telecommunications, hardware, data, agriculture and so on – on the rest of the world. If the US and EU can agree to common global (and non-Chinese) standards, Chinese firms will have to pay the cost of entering American and European markets rather than the other way round.

To some extent, the pursuit of these two mega-regional deals has reflected frustration at the lack of progress in the Doha Round of multilateral negotiations. This stalemate has been attributed to obstructionism by China and especially India, but even if that were true, it is only partially so. The Doha Round held few attractions for the US and its private-sector interests. In other words, even a successful conclusion of a Doha Round would not have detracted from the appeal of, nor obviated the perceived need for, initiatives such as the TPP and TTIP.

Economic benefits of the TPP and TTIP

Both PTAs being sought by Washington will confer benefits and impose costs in particular sectors. But it can safely be assumed that neither the TPP nor the TTIP will confer large benefits in a macroeconomic sense.

In the case of the TPP, the modest gains for the US stem from the asymmetric market opening. It is well known that most of the economic and/or welfare gains from trade liberalisation stem from a country's own liberalisation. Because the US is unlikely to undertake significant opening itself through the TPP, US consumers do not stand to reap large gains. The economic gains to the US will accrue in the form of rents to American producers in partner countries opening up their markets preferentially. The magnitude of these rents will depend on how protected those markets were in the first place. The big partner-country markets – Canada, Japan and Korea – already are relatively open, limiting the potential rents that US firms will reap. One, probably optimistic, estimate by Peter Petri and Michael Plummer suggests that the gains to the US in 2025 from a TPP including Japan, Mexico, Canada and Korea will be about 0.4% of GDP.[29]

Economic gains from the TTIP are also unlikely to be large, but for different and subtler reasons. Conventional trade barriers in both the US and EU are relatively small – with notable exceptions such as government procurement and air transport that are likely to remain exceptions. Where they are significant, their scope is narrow, as in agriculture. For these reasons, the TTIP cannot generate large economic gains measured as a share of the US economy.

What about the gains from regulatory harmonisation or convergence? The TTIP will focus to a great extent on addressing differences in regulation across the two jurisdictions. In agriculture, the EU favours strict safety and sanitary regulations – applying the 'precautionary principle' over the scientific risk assessment used in the US. In relation to data, the EU favours stricter standards to safeguard privacy and private rights, while the US prefers market-driven solutions. France seeks to protect its artistic heritage by way of an *exception culturelle* to free trade. In relation to protecting wines and spirits, the EU favours high levels of protection for certain geographical appellations (think of the block on producers outside the region calling their product 'champagne').

The economic/welfare calculus of regulatory convergence – if indeed that is going to happen under TTIP – is complicated.

If, to start with, each country's trade-off between regulation and liberalisation represents some kind of revealed collective preference, any departures altering that trade-off will have ambiguous consequences.

If the EU relaxes its safety regulations to allow in more US beef, EU beef-eaters will benefit; but they will also lose because they have in some sense been exposed to more risk. After all, this is why the stricter regulation existed in the first place (unless, of course, the regulation was pure protectionism even to begin with). Similarly, if the US strengthens protection for geographical appellations such as 'champagne', more French bubbly will benefit some American consumers but there will also be costs because access will be curtailed to New World bubbly no longer able to use the 'champagne' label). The bottom line is that by definition, the nature of integration between the US and EU will result in very small overall gains if regulations are properly accounted for. Therefore, given the nature of the two economies and the integration envisaged, any claims about large benefits are simply implausible.

Impact on China

In trade terms, China is the biggest prize, for two reasons. It is not only one of the world's largest and most dynamic markets, it is also one of the most protected. While China's formal trade barriers have come down sharply in manufacturing, barriers remain substantial in services and government procurement, and informal barriers are also extensive due to the actions of state trading enterprises. By contrast, US and EU markets are more open.

The strongest pressure on China to liberalise will be domestic. There are signs that the new leadership wants to rebalance and reform its economy, especially the state-owned and services sectors, to secure durably high and high-quality growth. This is unilateral opening.

So how could the US influence China's market opening in a bargaining environment? It could do so in three ways. Firstly, the US could say: 'You (China) open your markets and we will open ours.' This is the standard mercantilist reciprocity bargain. But this bargain runs up against the problem of asymmetry: the US is very open and has not a lot to offer, while China is closed. In this exchange, China has the overwhelming balance of mercantilist bargaining power. So, shifting power militates against this strategy.

Secondly, the US could say: 'You (China) open your markets, otherwise we will close ours.' However, this is dangerously belligerent. It is protectionist in tone and intent, and would go against the spirit of the current liberal trading system, which China will surely exploit. So, ideas and power will both militate against this approach.

The third alternative is to impose costs on China indirectly – not by raising American barriers but by lowering barriers in American, Asian and European markets in a discriminatory fashion to the disadvantage of Chinese firms. This is what the TPP and TTIP will achieve. They will indirectly inflict costs on China by worsening its competitive position in international markets.

China can respond in a variety of ways. It can offset its own disadvantage relative to American competition in Asia-Pacific markets by negotiating free-trade agreements of its own with countries in the region. Indeed, that is what it is doing. China has negotiated agreements with four countries already and the Regional Comprehensive Economic Partnership (RCEP) between ASEAN and six other countries (Australia, Japan, New Zealand, Korea, India and China) is aimed at widening this circle of free-trade agreements to parry similar American efforts.

But such agreements negotiated by China also impose a cost on American and European firms because in Chinese markets they are now disadvantaged relative to Asian firms. De facto, the TPP and TTIP combined with Chinese responses to them, amount to an elaborate trade war by proxy.

How this war ends will depend a lot on China. If it chafes under this strategy of containment, it could prolong the war by targeting the US, for example by negotiating trade agreements with Korea and Japan that would create even more discrimination against American business.

On the other hand, Chinese pragmatism might prevail. Seeking to avoid the impact of the TPP and TTIP on its own exports and economic trajectory, China could come to the negotiating table. The early evidence suggests that Japan's entry into TPP negotiations may have altered China's approach to the agreement. Beijing quickly recognised the economic losses it would suffer as a result, and became much more forthcoming about its own market opening. This change in approach is manifest in China's willingness to negotiate a bilateral investment treaty agreement with the US; its efforts to join the Trade in Services Agreement (TISA) negotiations in Geneva; its more nuanced and less obstructionist approach to the Information Technology Agreement (ITA-2) in Geneva; its willingness to join negotiations on environmental trade; and even a seeming willingness to join the TPP itself.

Especially if China wants to liberalise for domestic reasons – and there are increasing signs pointing in that direction – it might want to repeat Premier Zhu Rongji's tactics when China joined the WTO more than a decade ago. By negotiating with its larger trading partners, China could seek to extract concessions for liberalisation that it wants to undertake anyway.

Meanwhile, the TPP and TTIP negotiations are in considerable flux in the US. The Democrats ruled out a grant of trade-promotion authority until after the Congressional elections in November 2014. But even afterwards it has not become clear that the US as a whole can muster the political support to pursue negotiations. There are multiple ironies and paradoxes here.

The fact that the US even initiated the TPP and TTIP as an attempt to contain China was surprising given the shifting power balance between the two. It was also remarkable that it did so when the climate for pursuing trade liberalisation was extremely poor, around the twentieth anniversary of the North American Free Trade Agreement (NAFTA), a lightning rod for the many grievances against globalisation. On both power and ideology grounds, the TPP and TTIP were bold gambits, partially defying underlying trends.

Another irony is that the US is retreating, or being forced to retreat, from these initiatives at the very point that they seem to be 'working' vis-à-vis China. Even in decline, the US seems to have vestigial power to wield effectively against its ascendant rival.

The politics of the TPP and TTIP in the US will depend a lot on the China dimension. The economic effects of these two initiatives will be perceived in the political arena as either marginally negative or neutral. The TPP will fare slightly better than the TTIP because it involves more asymmetric liberalisation. Fewer domestic interests, whether producers or labour, will be threatened by the TPP. And some producer interests, namely American exporters, will gain. The politics of the TTIP, on the other hand, will be ambiguous because some of the liberalisation it entails will threaten domestic US producers. Moreover, because of regulatory changes, resistance will also come from domestic agencies, attempting to ward off encroachment on, and dilution of, their authority.

On foreign-policy grounds too, the TPP will fare better than the TTIP. The TPP could contain China both economically and politically. This will strike a chord with an instinctively insular

Congress wary of China. The TTIP may not have the same resonance in Congress because China will not be explicitly targeted.

Conclusion

Many questions surround the two major developments under way in trade: challenges to globalisation in the West and impending mega-regionalism in trade deals. Can the idea of globalisation survive the prevailing economic forces that are restricting growth in the US and Europe, straining public balance sheets, eroding the tax base necessary to sustain the political consensus for globalisation, and causing worsening inequality, especially in the US? Should one be sanguine, based on the way the US almost shrugged off the China shock, or should one be more cautious because of ominous forces that threaten globalisation?

As it pursues two major mega-regional deals, will the US achieve its objective of containing China politically and inducing it to open up its markets economically? Or will its actions provoke frictions within, and lead to fragmentation of, the multinational trading system? Will the status quo power achieve its ends or will the rising power mount a challenge?

Where all of this leaves the WTO and multilateralism is, of course, of pressing concern. It is not that the WTO and multilateralism have become irrelevant. An increasing number of countries, including Russia, want to join the WTO. Its dispute-settlement system functions effectively, its basic rules are broadly respected. The question is whether it retains its relevance as a key forum for facilitating further liberalisation or transforms itself into an institution that serves mainly as a court of trade law and an overseer of expanding regional trade.

Notes

1 Arvind Subramanian and Martin Kessler, 'The Hyper-globalisation of Trade and Its Future', in Shahrokh Fardoust (ed.), *Towards a Better Global Economy* (Oxford: Oxford University Press, 2014).

2 The other four characteristics highlighted in our article were: the dematerialisation of globalisation (the importance of services); democratic globalisation (the widespread embrace of openness); criss-crossing globalisation (the similarity of north–south and south–north trade and investment flows); and the decline of barriers to trade in goods but the continued existence of high barriers to trade in services.

3 David Hummels, Jun Ishii and Kei-Mu Yi, 'The Nature and Growth of Vertical Specialisation in World Trade', *Journal of International Economics*, vol. 54, no. 1, 2001, pp. 75–96.

4 Richard Baldwin, 'Trade and Industrialisation after Globalisation's 2nd Unbundling: How Building and Joining a Supply Chain Are Different and Why It Matters', Working Paper 17716, National Bureau of Economic Research (Cambridge, MA: National Bureau of Economic Research, 2011).

5 John Maynard Keynes, *The Economics Consequences of the Peace* (New York: Harcourt, Brace and Howe, 1920), p.11.

6 Kevin H. O'Rourke and Jeffrey G. Williamson, *Globalisation and History: The Evolution of a Nineteenth-Century Atlantic Economy* (Cambridge, MA: The MIT Press, 1999); Jeffry A. Frieden, *Global Capitalism: Its Fall and Rise in the Twentieth Century* (New York: W.W. Norton, 2006); Douglas Irwin, *Trade Policy Disaster: Lessons from the 1930s*, (Cambridge, MA: The MIT Press, 2011).

7 Subramanian and Kessler, 'The Hyper-globalisation of Trade and Its Future'.

8 *Ibid.*

9 *Ibid.*

10 Robert Lawrence, *Regionalism, Multilateralism and Deeper Integration* (Washington DC: Brookings Institution, 1996).

11 Pew Research Center, 'Americans Are of Two Minds on Trade – More Trade, Mostly Good; Free Trade Pacts, Not So', 9 November 2010.

12 See the discussion in Subramanian and Kessler (2014) for the views of economists Paul Samuelson, Paul Krugman and Larry Summers. For a response to Samuelson, see Jagdish Bhagwati, Arvind Panagariya and T. N. Srinivasan, 'The Muddles over Outsourcing', *Journal of Economic Perspectives*, vol. 18, no. 4, Fall 2004, pp. 93–114.

13 Thomas Piketty and Emmanuel Saez, 'Income Inequality in the United States, 1913–1998', *Quarterly Journal of Economics*, vol. 118, no. 1, February 2003, pp. 1–41.

14 Ron Haskins, Julia Isaacs, and Isabel Sawhill, 'Getting Ahead or Losing Ground: Economic Mobility in America', Brookings Institution, Economic Mobility Project Report, February 2008.

15 See 'World Economic Outlook: Legacies, Clouds, Uncertainties',

(Washington DC: IMF, 2014), http://www.imf.org/external/pubs/ft/weo/2014/02.

16 Dani Rodrik, 'Why Do More Open Economies Have Bigger Governments?', *Journal of Political Economy*, vol. 106, no. 5, 1998, pp. 997–1,032.

17 David Autor, David Dorn and Gordon Hanson, 'The China Syndrome: Local Labor Market Effects of Import Competition in the United States', *American Economic Review*, vol. 103, no. 6, 2013, pp. 2,121–68.

18 Larry Summers, 'America needs to make a new case for trade', *Financial Times*, 27 April 2008.

19 Thomas Piketty, *Capital in the Twenty-First Century* (Cambridge, MA: Harvard University Press, 2014).

20 Paul Krugman, 'Trade and Wages, Reconsidered', *Brookings Papers on Economic Activity*, Economic Studies Programme, Brookings Institution, vol. 39, no. 1, Spring 2008, pp. 103–54.

21 John Gerard Ruggie, *Constructing the World Polity* (London: Routledge, 1998).

22 Barry Eichengreen and Douglas Irwin, 'The Protectionist Temptation: Lessons from the Great Depression for Today', *Vox* (the Centre for Economic Policy Research's policy portal), 17 March 2009.

23 Autor, Dorn and Hanson, 'The China Syndrome'.

24 Richard Baldwin and Simon Evenett, *The Collapse of Global Trade, Murky Protectionism and the Crisis: Recommendations for the G20* (London: Centre for Economic Policy Research, 2009).

25 The Reagan era witnessed the greatest upsurge in trade barriers in the postwar period; see I.M. Destler, *American Trade Politics*, (New York: New York University Press, 1992).

26 In Subramanian and Kessler (2014), we plot the same data but for a shorter period for which value-added trade data can be computed. Gross exports overstate value-added exports for China, but they overstate them even more for Mexico.

27 Calibrated by per capita GDP, it was even greater, and one reason to do this is that trade with low-income countries is of the Heckscher–Ohlin variety (which theorises that countries will export products that use cheap resources and production methods they have in abundance and import products using resources and factors of production scarce in their territory). It therefore imposes greater domestic political costs than, say, trade in similar goods between countries at similar levels of development, especially because these costs are disproportionately borne by unskilled labour, which competes more directly with foreign imports. Paul Krugman has elaborated on the reasons for intra-industry trade posing fewer political problems than Heckscher–Ohlin trade; see Paul Krugman, 'Growing World Trade: Causes and Consequences', *Brookings Papers on Economic Activity*, vol. 1995, no. 1, 25th Anniversary Issue (1995), pp. 327–77.

28 See Subramanian and Kessler, 'The Hyper-globalisation of Trade and Its Future', Appendix, Table A.1. In this table, the figures for

China are recomputed based on value-added trade data (we cannot do the same for the Mexican and Japanese shocks, which would bias the comparison in favour of understating the China shock). The size of the Chinese shock declines, but it remains orders of magnitude larger than the earlier shocks from Japan and Mexico.

29 Peter A. Petri and Michael G. Plummer, 'The Trans-Pacific Partnership and Asia-Pacific Integration: Policy Implications', *Policy Brief*, nos. 12–16, Peterson Institute for International Economics, June 2012.

CHAPTER THREE

Is trade multilateralism being threatened by regionalism?

Pascal Lamy

Since the creation of the General Agreement on Tariffs and Trade (GATT) in 1947, the multilateral trading system has ranked as one of the shining successes of international cooperation. Recently, it was shown to have great resilience in containing protectionist pressures during the 2008 global financial and economic crisis.[1] This was in marked contrast to events surrounding the Great Depression of the early 1930s, when defensive and increasingly hostile trade blocs arose in the interwar period.

However, with the stalling of the Doha Round of trade talks from 2008, the most active trade negotiations have been of a bilateral nature. Even if many of these negotiations have not yet resulted in agreements, they have often overlapped and interacted, creating a trade landscape defined less by clear-cut choices between regionalism and multilateralism – or discrimination and non-discrimination – than by the complex interplay among multiple trade regimes. Much ink has been spilled over their positive or negative impact on multilateralism during the past decades.

More recently, several mega-regional trade negotiations have been initiated with an ambition of deeper integration in a broad range of provisions – including in trade in services, investment, competition and important regulatory areas – which are largely absent from the older generation of regional trade agreements (RTAs) negotiated before GATT became the World Trade Organisation (WTO) in 1995. These new mega-RTAs raise new challenges, and intensify the debate over the relationship between regionalism and multilateralism.

Leaving aside the geopolitical dimensions that preferential trade agreements (PTAs) may involve and focusing on the trade aspects, the question is whether PTAs threaten the benefits of multilateralism in trade regulation? Do they stimulate or hamper multilateralism?

'It depends' is the short answer to this question. So far, the increase in PTAs has resulted overall in a de facto convergence at the multilateral level. But whether this will continue is uncertain. It will depend on whether convergence between multilateralism and regionalism is organised or not.

Convergence between multilateralism and regionalism to date

Modern trade policy is based on a broad global consensus on three principles: that opening trade increases economic efficiency, fostering growth and, if properly coordinated with other policies, developing welfare; that non-discrimination, based on the principle of Most Favoured Nation (MFN) status, allows each country to exploit its comparative advantage; and that the stability and predictability of trade rules provides economic operators with a framework conducive to investment and development.

To maximise the combined effect of these principles, multilateralism in trade rules ensures an optimum, in a different manner to other avenues of regulating trade. Multilateralism is preferable not just because it is non-discriminatory, but also because bringing rules into the WTO makes for a greater level of transparency, enforceability and inclusiveness.[2] By creating a world that is driven by preordained policies and conduct rather than by reactionary behaviour, WTO rules help to level the playing field and reduce power asymmetries.

It is by definition discriminatory to establish specific contractual preferences both on WTO-plus issues – i.e., deeper integration in areas covered by the WTO such as industrial and agricultural tariffs, technical barriers to trade, intellectual property, public procurement – and on WTO-extra issues not covered by the WTO, such as competition policy and investment. Unilateral preferences, such as the US African Growth and Opportunity Act (AGOA) or the EU Generalised Scheme of Preferences (GSP) for developing countries, usually have their own specific conditionalities in areas such as environment or social standards. Moreover, because they are periodically reviewed – the so-called 'graduation' technique – they remain uncertain.

Even before the start of the negotiation of mega-regional trade agreements extending their ambition to deeper integration across a broader range of issues, many smaller bilateral agreements had already entered into force: close to 300 in 2010 and 377 by January 2014. Despite the conclusion of the Uruguay Round in 1994, bringing not only agriculture and environment but also services and intellectual property issues within the realm of the WTO, subsequent ministerial meetings demonstrated that multilateral agreements would be much more difficult to achieve in contentious areas such as competition policy or even government procurement. Negotiators took for granted that it would be easier to achieve trade and investment liberalisation in the new areas among smaller groups of trading partners, or on a bilateral basis.

At the turn of the century, the case was made for 'competitive liberalisation'. According to this theory the multiplication of bilateral trade preferences would incentivise those not yet on the liberalisation merry-go-round to overcome their resistance and jump on board.

The question of whether these arrangements complement or compete with multilateralism is thus not a new question. Whether RTAs are stepping stones or stumbling blocks to multilateralism has been a matter for debate in trade literature for decades: could burgeoning regionalism signal a weakening of international commitment to open trade, and foreshadow a return to a more fragmented trading system? Alternatively, could the willingness of some countries to move further and faster than others in trade rule-making have a positive domino effect, encouraging the pace of multilateral cooperation?

Judgement on that issue does not rest on the merits of various frameworks or parameters. What matters at the end of the day is the reduction of obstacles to trade and whether the agreements in question contribute to the removal of those barriers.

So long as trade agreements were about addressing traditional trade obstacles such as tariffs, any path to opening trade through increased market access (multilateral, bilateral or unilateral) resulted in more convergence than divergence. The fear of 'trade diversion' seldom materialised.

Bilateral preferential tariffs are often more efficient in terms of market opening, as they operate via applied tariffs whereas many WTO bound tariffs are ceilings not to be exceeded, but they often remain significantly higher than the applied tariff.[3]

Trade preferences are self-eroding: the more you provide, the less impact they have. In fact, the share of trade taking place under preferential regimes is small and shrinking: only 16% of world trade is preferential and less than 2% of current world imports are eligible for preferential tariffs where preference margins are 10% or more.[4] This is largely because, despite the increase of PTAs in recent years, 84% of trade flows fall under the multilateral non-discriminatory principle of MFN status. Furthermore, for most traded items, their MFN rates are already low or zero, which limits the scope for granting preferences.

'Sensitive' sectors – such as agriculture or food items and labour-intensive manufactured products such as footwear and textiles – are often excluded from liberalisation in bilateral agreements, notwithstanding the letter of GATT/WTO Article XXIV. Smaller economies that export a narrow set of those commodities frequently avoid integrating those sectors into bilateral agreements. And there is a possibility that these remaining more substantial preference margins will be eroded over time as the countries of destination enter into more PTAs.

In some areas, however, the coexistence of regionalism and multilateralism may not have worked as well, as is the case for rules of origin (determining a country from which a product comes) and dispute settlement.

Rules of origin are effective tools for enforcing bilateral preferences, as they oblige traders to show a 'passport' for goods so that the preference is effectively granted to the country of origin and not to another – Bhagwati's 'spaghetti bowl effect'.[5] But rules of origin can also impose an additional impediment to trade when they distort the effectiveness of such preferences.

The use of more solid and far-reaching dispute-settlement mechanisms in free-trade agreements – shifting from the political or diplomatic approach to a quasi-judicial model based on an ad hoc adjudicating body and a standing appellate tribunal – has raised fears of overlap or variances with the WTO's Dispute Settlement Body (DSB).

To date there has been no clear evidence of inconsistency between decisions emanating from FTA dispute-settlement tribunals and the jurisprudence of the WTO dispute-settlement panels and the Appellate Body. Very few dispute-settlement mechanisms under RTAs exclude recourse to WTO settlement procedures. Many instead, leave the choice of forum to the party initiating a dispute; and cases arising under the covered agreements of the WTO are in practice much more commonly brought before the WTO than resolved through reference to the FTA's dispute-settlement mechanism.

The WTO option is particularly reassuring for smaller countries. Article 9 of the WTO's Dispute Settlement Understanding facilitates grouping of complainants. In addition, if supervision of implementation and sanctions is possible everywhere, WTO offers the added value of arbitration over sanctions, cross-retaliation[6] and multilateral surveillance. The WTO dispute mechanism is compulsory and mandatory: almost 30 RTAs offer the option of asking the director-general of the WTO to nominate panellists for an RTA dispute, where the parties to the dispute cannot agree on the choice of panellists.

RTAs are a good forum for discussions and are conducive to deeper commitments on issues such as competition or investment. But the WTO offers superior dispute settlement, as well as the institutional support provided by the WTO Secretariat and cost advantages.

According to the WTO's *World Trade Report 2011*, recent regional and multilateral initiatives in fact represent complementary aspects of an increasingly complex and sophisticated global trade architecture – one in which bilateral, regional, cross-regional and multilateral agreements coexist and cohere in a kind of 'multispeed' or 'variable geometry' system.[7]

Yet, as rule-making in international trade moves beyond the reduction of tariff barriers into the challenges of deeper policy integration, these more comprehensive and complex agreements tend to blur the meaning of discrimination.

The changing nature of trade

The development of a new generation of free-trade agreements, the so-called mega-RTAs, may well have a more significant negative impact on global trade regulation. Three such agreements under negotiation have already been mentioned in this book: the Trans-Pacific Partnership (TPP) between the United States and 11 other countries (Australia, Brunei, Chile, Canada, Japan, Malaysia, Mexico, New Zealand, Peru, Singapore and Vietnam); the Transatlantic Trade and Investment Partnership (TTIP) between the US and the European Union (EU); and the Regional Comprehensive Economic Partnership (RCEP) between the ten ASEAN members and six other Asian countries (Australia, China, India, Japan, New Zealand and South Korea). In addition, there is the Trilateral Agreement negotiated between China, Japan and Korea, as well as the bilateral trade and investment pact being discussed between the EU and Japan.

The specificity of these mega-RTAs lies in their size, but more fundamentally in their level of ambition, namely deeper integration that follows the evolution of global production networks and reflects the relative decrease of the importance of tariff protection.

Taking advantage of the most cost-effective and added-value locations, companies have increasingly tended to substitute the 'Made at home' label with a new 'Made in the world' sticker. The import content of exports keeps growing, making the relationship between the two increasingly organic; it has grown from an average worldwide of approximately 20% in the 1990s, to 40% today, and could rise to 60% by 2030.[8] Intermediate goods, which today represent an average of 50% to 60% of total merchandise trade,[9] will continue to play an increasing role in global production chains.

The expansion of these production chains has led trade negotiators to expand the perimeter of mega-RTA negotiations into WTO-plus provisions (which are largely regulatory in nature) and WTO-extra provisions.

A growing proportion of obstacles to trade today are differences in standards and norms of production. The measures adopted in each country to protect the consumer from risks (standards, norms, certification systems) often differ, presenting exporters with a patchwork of different regulatory regimes, and perhaps an unlevel playing field.

Rather than being protectionist measures, standards play an increasing role in market integration. They allow suppliers and clients to better link up on the same supply chain. Suppliers tend by themselves to adopt private standards that signal to lead firms that they could be desirable suppliers. Coordinating private standards with public standards would therefore be a market-integration driver.

Mutual recognition of conformity and certification systems (for instance, to avoid a single product having to be tested twice) and the simplification of the rules of origin would greatly help in reducing the costs of regulation.

It is therefore no surprise that the economies of scale to be gained from regulatory convergence are now at the heart of the new mega-trade deals, especially those among large economies with sophisticated regulatory systems. The most obvious case is the transatlantic free-trade agreement, the TTIP. If the negotiations were to succeed, 80% of the expected benefits would be derived from the economies of scale and reduced transactions costs gained from regulatory convergence, as well as from the opening of trade in services and public procurement.[10]

Yet, this change in the nature of the obstacles to trade, with the growing importance of regulations and standards over tariffs, will decisively transform at least four major parameters of the negotiation of the new generation of trade agreements.[11]

Levelling, not eliminating, differences

Whereas the name of the game used to be tariff reduction, leading eventually to tariff elimination, addressing regulatory discrepancies is different. It is not about eliminating the measures themselves, because elimination of precautionary measures makes no sense; it is about levelling the differences in these measures. This doesn't mean a striving for uniformity. Because any attempt to homogenise societal or collective preferences is intrusive, the question remains how far we can go. Cooperation in regulatory convergence can only be about avoiding unnecessary friction or unwarranted discrimination. In many cases, differences in non-tariff measures may simply be incidental – a matter of form – driven by the shadow of past practice. Differences may also result from a lack of technical or enforcement capacity. Those incidental divergences can thus be tackled either through harmonisation or mutual recognition of each other's standards or conformity-assessment procedures.

Negotiation changes hands

The leading players in regulatory convergence are not the same as for tariff negotiations. Considering the technicality and complexity of the regulatory field, the considerable experience built up by official negotiators in the field of domestic producers' protection (whether tariffs, quantitative restrictions or subsidies) needs to be complemented by the additional expertise of the regulatory agencies governing consumer protection. They need to work hand in hand, which is not a given.

Taking consumer concerns into account

The political economy of regulatory convergence is radically different from that surrounding tariff negotiation. Previous negotiations have been of greater concern to producers, because tariffs barriers are designed to shield them from competition from imports; regulatory convergence attracts greater attention from consumers. They may fear that the level of precaution guaranteed by the current norms and standards based on so-called 'collective preferences'[12] could be lowered by any regulatory convergence. Such a convergence would therefore run counter to their interests as consumers. They would tend to view the final agreements as less beneficial to them than to producers, so negotiations would take place in a more combative public arena.

Trade negotiators previously had to overcome domestic producers' resistance to more competition, while drawing support from consumers benefiting from better prices. They now have to face consumers fearing a reduction in the level of protections, while gaining support from producers anticipating economies of scale. This reverse challenge has consequences for various processes whose ultimate purpose is to ensure legitimacy, and for the eventual buy-in of various stakeholders, through transparency, consultation and public debate.

Consumer and other standards allow no special treatment

In terms of market access, GATT and the WTO have long provided for 'special and differential treatment' for developing countries, to afford them a higher level of protection for development purposes. This has led to asymmetries in trade opening in both multilateral and preferential trade regimes.

However, in the area of precaution – in setting standards and consumer protections – markets do not afford special treatment: if the protection of domestic producers can be graduated and import levels accepted as a function of the country of origin of an import, the protection of consumers does not tolerate even partial market access to preferential imports: precaution cannot be 'graduated'. Whether a product matches a standard is a yes–no question, not a question of how much.

For these reasons, the ongoing transformation in the nature of obstacles to trade – and in ways and means to reduce them – raises new issues around the relationship between a multilateral, non-discriminatory regime, and a bilateral or regional preferential regime. Assuming a successful outcome of those new agreements, the past synergy between multilateral and regional approaches to trade opening is less obvious for the future, as there is no more guarantee that bilateral convergence would lead to multilateral convergence: whether intended or not, harmonisation of regulatory standards can have a 'preferential' effect if it effectively creates a regional regulatory 'bloc' that benefits insiders more than outsiders.

In this context, the overlapping membership of the mega-RTAs under negotiation could only be a minor factor in convergence, as the content of their respective agendas differs. When it comes to regulation, the RCEP is less ambitious in scope than the TPP and much less ambitious than the TTIP, whose main objective concerns regulatory convergence.

Therefore, the risk for the future is that the multilateral playing field will be overshadowed by a proliferation of divergent regulatory regimes,[13] with the establishment of 'regulatory blocs' disrupting global supply chains and leading to major trade diversion – in other words scattering the trade regime and undermining the WTO's centrality.

The potential impact of twenty-first-century regionalism

Research into regionalism, with its almost exclusive focus on tariffs and quotas, provides only limited evidence on the implications for standards.[14] The TTIP and the RCEP are still in the early stages of negotiations that will last years if not decades, and TPP negotiations have only been under way since December 2010. Therefore, the jury is out on three questions that will determine the future of the global trade regime.

Firstly, how far can bilateral regulatory convergence happen in order to address 'new' precaution-related obstacles to trade? It is not easy at this stage to evaluate which elements of regulatory convergence may be successfully included in the TPP beyond intellectual property, state-owned enterprises or public procurement. The diversity of the countries involved in that agreement will certainly not help in negotiating convergence. TTIP negotiations will also be technically and politically complex, because citizens on both sides of the Atlantic tend to firmly hold to the risk-management process adopted in their own country – whether that be the more 'after the fact' approach towards civil liability on the American side or the more 'before the event' one on the European side, which lead to different levels of precaution. Different perceptions of risk will play an important role here too.

Secondly, how will any bilateral regulatory convergence that emerges later morph into multilateral regulatory convergence? To ensure a certain degree of coherence between the regulatory chapters in various agreements, it would be helpful for those agreements to remain relatively open to third countries. This would greatly contribute to a future multilateralisation, but it would require that participants agree on rules that do not impede access to their blocs and do not contradict the fundamental principles of equity and openness of international trade.

The multilateralisation of regulatory convergence will notably depend on whether bilateral and other preferential agreements produce full regulatory convergence, via harmonisation, or whether they actually produce regulatory compatibility primarily through conditional mutual recognition. The first option would enable producers everywhere to take advantage of economies of scale. However, in some cases, the harmonised standard could be more stringent than some countries' original standards. With mutual recognition, the partners would accept each other's standards or conformity-assessment procedures, allowing firms to adhere to the less stringent requirements in each area. If the policy were extended to third-country firms, it could have a powerful liberalising impact.[15] Unlike harmonisation, which demands a lengthy negotiation process, mutual recognition is more flexible and easier to apply with regards to existing regulations because it does not have the same legal, financial or psychological implications.

However, mutual recognition is a more convenient option for negotiating partners with relatively similar initial standards. In addition, the partners would need to agree on opening the mutual-recognition policy to third-country firms by avoiding restrictive rules of origin – which, incidentally, are becoming less meaningful as it becomes harder to apply a nationality to a product. And mutual recognition cannot easily be made multilateral because it implies ongoing cooperation between regulators, and the greater the number of regulators involved in any cooperative venture, the more difficult it is to achieve consensus.

Thirdly, how will regionalism impact dispute settlement? Specific attention needs to be paid to the impact of the mega-RTAs here, as dispute-settlement mechanisms play a greater role in ever-tighter global economic integration, creating tensions between domestic sovereignty and a growing demand for rules preventing discrimination and protectionism.

The ambition of mega-RTAs to cover more WTO-plus issues – leading to potential disputes that cannot be brought before the WTO – raises new concerns over the possible fragmentation of dispute settlement in international trade. Countries can also try to stretch the scope of existing WTO provisions to include RTA matters in disputes submitted to the automatic WTO Dispute Settlement Body. It would be better for the DSB to decide on the scope of the WTO provision concerned.

The increase of cross-border investments has contributed, along with transnational supply chains, to a change in the substance of trade agreements, and is putting the spotlight on Investor–State Dispute Settlement (ISDS) issues. There is intense debate over the inclusion in mega-RTAs of a specific ISDS enabling foreign investors to sue host governments in third-party arbitration tribunals for treatment that allegedly fails to meet certain standards and results in a loss of asset values. How does one maintain a good balance between non-discriminatory treaty compliance and domestic regulatory autonomy as far as this is concerned? Bolivia withdrew from the Convention on the Settlement of Investment Disputes between States and Nationals of Other States (the ICSID Convention) in 2007, followed by Ecuador in 2009 and Venezuela in 2012, and did not renew certain bilateral investment treaties containing an ISDS provision. Indonesia has also announced that it will not renew such treaties, while South Africa plans to withdraw from treaties containing ISDS mechanisms. Similar doubts have been expressed by various stakeholders in the TTIP.

Worst-case scenario or win–win situation?

As far as regulatory convergence is concerned, three types of potential relationship between future regional and multilateral trade regimes can be envisaged. The first could be described as a 'clash of the titans', in which a US–EU regulatory bloc faces a Chinese regulatory bloc, leading to a new form of fragmentation of global trade, with negative impacts for Africa, Latin America, Russia and others. In the second 'back to the future' scenario, TTIP negotiations reach a successful conclusion and are complemented by two bilateral agreements between Japan and the EU and Japan and the US (via the TPP), giving the norms and standards arising out of these agreements a dominant world position. This would return us to the twentieth-century dominance of the old industrial countries, with other trade partners aligning themselves with the leading norms and standards. In the third alternative, 'for global trade's sake', regulatory convergence would be overseen at the global level for the benefit of all. To prevent unnecessary trade tensions and to ensure the potential of world growth, twenty-first-century global trade governance would be updated with a common strategy to manage regulatory convergence.

This third scenario is still far from ideal and would really require two important initiatives to be undertaken at an early stage, while current regulatory convergence negotiations remain open. Firstly, giving the WTO a supervisory role over regulatory convergence would help bring the subject into a multilateral framework. This enhanced WTO remit should also embrace convergence between public and private standards.[16] Secondly, the legal basis provided by GATT/WTO Article XXIV, which deals with discrimination resulting from tariff preferences, would need to be adapted to encompass regulatory preference. Relying on a mere interpretation of the original GATT Article XXIV for regulatory preferences would be insufficient.

Besides this, an important step would be to request WTO members to pursue a transparent approach in their negotiations. They should improve their record of observance of the transparency obligations in terms of trade policies, measures and data.[17] Sharing information is a key governing principle of multilateralism. Trade becomes less certain and stable when information is poorly distributed among interested parties. WTO members should thus be willing to consult their trading partners when negotiating, and to strengthen domestic dialogue among interested parties, including business, civil society and trade unions.

Greater transparency should also be extended to policy data complementing the WTO-mandated review of RTAs, which unfortunately remains below many WTO members' radars. A consortium of institutions – the International Centre for Trade and Sustainable Development, the Inter-American Development Bank, and the Asian Development Bank Institute – is now producing an 'RTA Exchange' to serve as a source of information and promote international dialogue, deeper analysis and information sharing. Looking ahead, the WTO and the Organisation for Economic Cooperation and Development (OECD) could also contribute further research and analysis in several areas, including by highlighting provisions in RTAs that go above or beyond WTO commitments and that might be able to be multilateralised.[18]

The work of the Asia-Pacific Economic Cooperation (APEC) in developing best practices for PTAs could also serve as an example of how to move forward. As Baldwin and Thornton have suggested, the WTO could consider multi-tier multilateralisation.[19] The first tier, establishing voluntary best-practice guidelines for new RTAs, would encourage nations to consider the impact of their agreements on non-party WTO members and help reduce differences in wording (and thus interpretations) across RTAs. The hierarchy of best-practice guidelines – tailored to north–north, north–south and south–south RTAs – would allow for developmental differences. The second tier would involve agreeing on basic principles, including national treatment, third-party MFNs and transparency, already widely included in deeply integrated RTAs.

So far we can reasonably state that multilateralism has not been threatened by regionalism. But prospects for the future are more blurred. Whether or not a new generation of mega-RTAs based on regulatory convergence, such as the TTIP, will eventually lead to multilateral convergence depends on numerous parameters that have yet to be clarified. In other words, connecting the bilateral and the multilateral 'brains' of trade negotiators remains a challenge for the future.

Notes

1   Hiau Looi Kee, Cristina Neagu and Alessandro Nicita, *Is Protectionism on the Rise? Assessing National Trade Policies during the Crisis of 2008* (Washington DC: The World Bank, April 2010); and Matthieu Bussière, Emilia Pérez-Barreiro, Roland Straub and Daria Taglioni, 'Protectionist responses to the crisis: global trends and implications', Frankfurt, European Central Bank, Occasional Paper Series, no. 110, May 2010.

2   Global Forum on Trade, Paris, OECD, February 2014.

3   The difference between bound ceiling tariffs and applied tariffs is called 'water' in the WTO jargon.

4   *World Trade Report 2011 – The WTO and preferential trade agreements: From co-existence to coherence* (Geneva: World Trade Organisation, 2011).

5   The term 'spaghetti bowl effect' was first used by Jagdish Bhagwati, in 'US Trade Policy: The Infatuation with Free Trade Agreements', in Claude Barfield (ed.), *The Dangerous Obsession with Free Trade Areas* (Washington DC: American Enterprise Institute, 1995).

6   Cross-retaliation describes a situation where the complaining country retaliates by suspending concessions or other obligations under a sector or an agreement that has not been breached by the defending country.

7   *World Trade Report 2011*, p. 54.

8   Madhur Jha, Samantha Amerasinghe, Chidu Narayanan, John Calverley and Achilleas Chrysostomou, 'Global Trade Unbundled', Special Report, Standard Chartered Bank, 9 April 2014, p. 5, https://www.sc.com/en/resources/global-en/pdf/Research/2014/Global_trade_unbundled_10_04_14.pdf.

9   WTO, 'The Future of Trade: the Challenges of Convergence', Report of the Panel on Defining the Future of Trade convened by WTO director-general Pascal Lamy, Geneva, 2013, p. 22.

10 Joseph Francois (ed.), *Reducing Transatlantic Barriers to Trade and Investment. An Economic Assessment* (London: Centre for Economic Policy Research, 2013), p. vii.

11 Elvire Fabry, Giorgio Garbasso and Romain Pardo, 'The TTIP Negotiations: A Pirandello Play', Synthesis Report for the Notre Europe – Jacques Delors Institute/European Policy Centre, January 2014.

12 Pascal Lamy, *The Geneva Consensus: Making Trade Work for All* (Cambridge: Cambridge University Press, 2013).

13 *Ibid.*, p. 177.

14 For an estimation of the trade-diversion impact of the TTIP on third countries, see Francois, *Reduc-*

ing Transatlantic Barriers to Trade and Investment; and Gabriel Felbermayr, Benedikt Heid and Sybille Lehwald, 'Transatlantic Trade and Investment Partnership (TTIP): Who benefits from a free trade deal?', Report for the Bertelsmann Foundation, published by Global Economic Dynamics, 2013.

15 Aaditya Mattoo, 'An EU–US trade deal: Good or bad for the rest of the world?', *Vox* (the Centre for Economic Policy Research's policy portal), 13 October 2013.

16 WTO, 'The Future of Trade: The Challenges of Convergence'.

17 *Ibid.*, p. 6.

18 Global Forum on Trade, February 2014.

19 Richard Baldwin and Phil Thornton, *Multilateralising Regionalism: Ideas for a WTO Action Plan on Regionalism* (London: Centre for Economic Policy Research, 2008).

CHAPTER FOUR

Trade, development and developmental regionalism

Supachai Panitchpakdi

Multilateralism is experiencing dramatic shifts in almost all areas of the global economy involving trade, investment and the environment, as well as in the institutions of global governance. These tectonic shifts are being generated by the rise and decline of economic powers, which is being accompanied by a certain belligerent geopolitical repositioning. In the arena of world trade we find ourselves at a somewhat Alice-in-Wonderland fork in the road, where Alice, not knowing where she wants to go, is told by the Cheshire Cat that it doesn't matter which path she chooses.

For more than half a century the world trading system was driven by a group of like-minded countries, giving the system a semblance of leadership. From 1947 to 1979, during the first seven rounds of multilateral trade negotiations, the industrial nations together nudged the General Agreement on Tariffs and Trade (GATT) to lower industrial tariffs to below 5% on average. To avoid political roadblocks, however, they agreed not to make any inroads into farm trade.

Indeed, it opened a Pandora's box when the lengthy eighth trade round launched in Uruguay in 1986 began tackling new and diverse areas such as farm trade, intellectual property rights and trade-related investment. The GATT leadership of developed countries could only bring that round to a conclusion after a compromise agreement on farm trade called the Blair House Accord.[1] That accord was presented to other GATT members as a 'take it or leave it' solution. Of course the membership took it, and finally concluded the round in 1994.

The first trade round under the World Trade Organisation (WTO) that replaced GATT – the Doha Round or Doha Development Agenda (DDA) – was launched in 2001 with great difficulty, with consensus on the launch only reached after the initial five-day conference was extended into a sixth. For the first time developing countries demonstrated their new power by inserting the word 'development' into the trade agenda. This may now seem like an omen, because a 'round' is meant to have a completion date while an 'agenda' can be pursued indefinitely. Thirteen years on, debates still rage as to whether the negotiations under this agenda have lived up to the 'development' name. A lack of leadership has become clear, resulting in our Alice-in-Wonderland moment in which the agenda drifts on without any pointers as to where and how the negotiations can successfully end.

By 2005, the dysfunctional WTO Quad of trading powers – the US, EU, Japan and Canada – had been replaced by a Group of Five, with the US and EU joined by China, Brazil and India. This G5 moved the agenda forward and appeared to have some sort of end in sight, particularly at the ministerial meeting in Geneva in 2008. However, ultimately, their talks broke down. The problem is that equitable burden-sharing between advanced and developing countries, required to deepen trade liberalisation, has not been achieved.

On the one hand, advanced members would like to see more liberalisation by emerging economies, particularly in trade in manufactured goods and services. On the other hand, developing countries apparently do not consider that there have been adequate development contributions from the advanced economies in the areas of farm trade (including cotton), services (mobility of people) and some areas of special and differential treatment. The decisions taken at the Ninth WTO Ministerial Conference at Bali in December 2013, where some agreement was reached on certain basic principles in trade facilitation, could be viewed as a positive step aimed at keeping the DDA alive. But it is insufficient to take the whole agenda to completion, and the fate of the DDA seems to hang in the balance.

Against this background, three important questions have arisen, answers to which will be crucial in determining the future direction of the multilateral trading system. They are:

1. Since the WTO deals only with trade and cannot become a World Economic Organisation, how can it cope with an increasing number of elements going beyond pure trade or market access, such as the exchange-rate regime, balance of trade measured on the basis of value addition, investment policy, social and environmental policy, and so on?

2. Can trade be more organically linked to inclusive development through aid-for-trade, Trade-Related Aspects of Intellectual Property Rights (TRIPS) and public-health agreements, trade-and-technology and trade-and-employment creation (and maybe also trade-and-skill specialisation as prescribed by traditional trade theory)?

3. Would multilateral rule-making, the real core of the WTO's remit, be diluted by the emergence of not just regional trade agreements (RTAs) but the more sophisticated and all-encompassing twenty-first-century RTAs

that combine economic integration with economic partnership to acquire a geopolitical dimension?

The challenge of traditional regionalism

In reality, the urge to conclude bilateral or regional trade deals is not due to the lack of progress on the multilateral front. More than 500 RTAs were formed even before the WTO came into existence and 300 have been registered with the WTO. In the noughties, several RTAs were embarked upon, including by the US, before there was any concern over the slow progress of the DDA. When Doha talks began to stall after 2008, there was still little take-up for the effort to forge a closer transatlantic trade deal; this only got a serious boost in 2012.

One can lampoon the trade scene even during globalisation's heyday as one in which national leaders would be constantly travelling from one summit to another, signing off concluding statements full of platitudes about the importance of free trade and the necessity of completing the DDA trade round, before flying off to sign yet another RTA. As leaders' summits became more frequent, their marginal utility only declined further, making no real impact on real trade negotiations.

Trade ministers would ritually fly into Geneva or some other select venue for mini-ministerial meetings criticised by those not attending. No progress would be made as everybody waited for someone else to make the first move, the first contribution. Sometimes trade ministers would only show up to part of the WTO mini-ministerial meeting because they had to get away to attend a more important bilateral or regional trade meeting. All the while, WTO trade ambassadors would burn the midnight oil in Geneva to no avail.

Often countries have joined the preferential trade agreement (PTA) bandwagon for reasons of political expediency, claiming they have thereby gained trade competitiveness against their counterparts while in fact pursuing geopolitical or domestic political goals. Many RTAs and PTAs have been signed as a gesture to regional and domestic politics and as so-called acts of good-neighbourliness, while having no real economic content and not being based on any real economic analysis of their consequences.

If the number of trade deals were to be an index of trade openness, the African and South American continents should be among the most open and liberal, with a high percentage of intra-regional trade. But there is greater regional trade integration in Asia, where intra-regional trade accounts for 55% of total trade, despite a lower number of RTAs and PTAs than in South America and Africa, where intra-regional trade accounts for 15% and 10% of total trade respectively. Various empirical studies have come to the conclusion that PTAs do not necessarily contribute to trade liberalisation.[2]

PTAs are normally concluded not with the basic WTO principle of including 'substantially all trade' but with the intent of drawing up a long exclusion or negative list. The so-called 'spaghetti bowl' or 'noodle bowl' effects of PTAs[3] are most often referred to in respect of the confusion caused by the criss-crossing rules, regulations and standards spawned by competing and overlapping free trade and regional trade agreements. These get complicated by rules-of-origin provisions in RTAs and PTAs. All of these have acted as constraints on regional economic integration and trade rather than as a contribution towards it.

In the end, autonomous liberalisation has repeatedly proved to be the most meaningful way of opening up an economy, as countries can conveniently determine their own policy space and sequencing, and need not be involved in complex trade-offs with counterparties. However, RTAs and PTAs remain the flavour of our times in trade negotiations, so it's worth considering several of them further to realise that none of them is perfect.

The 28-member European Union (EU) is the 'mother of all regional integration'. From its foundations in the 1950s, it has contributed to 'peace in our time' on the continent and one can never ignore its geopolitical significance. However, there are plenty of things about Europe today that other countries would not wish to emulate, including the bloc's average 10% unemployment rate (with 24–26% joblessness in Spain and Greece, where youth unemployment tops 50%).[4] The sovereign-debt crisis within the EU, which has forced the European Central Bank and the International Monetary Fund to intervene, the doubtful quality of Europe's financial institutions, and a persistent deflationary environment resembling 1990s Japan are also unenviable characteristics.

The North American Free Trade Agreement (NAFTA) between the United States, Canada and Mexico celebrated its twentieth anniversary in 2014. Perhaps if it had been as successful as its supporters suggest, its members would not all be involved in negotiations to form a new Trans-Pacific Partnership (TPP)? For Mexico, for example, NAFTA has been neither an unmitigated disaster nor a complete success. It has contributed to Mexico's competitiveness in the US market, especially in the face of an onslaught from the Asian tiger economies, but it has contributed little to Mexico's development. Data show that the Mexican economy enjoyed better growth rates, on average, in the decade before NAFTA than during it. GDP per capita rose by only 0.9% per annum on average from 1994 to 2013, ranking number 18 out of 20 Latin American countries.[5] The level of poverty is essentially unchanged, with 52.3% of the population living in poverty in 2012 compared to 52.4% in 1994.[6] Besides this lack of development, Mexico has been infected by every economic malaise from its large neighbour to the north, from those surrounding the US Federal Reserve's interest-rate increase in 1994, the dotcom crash of 2001 and the stock-market bust of 2000–02, to that of the great recession of 2008–09 caused by the US subprime mortgage crisis.

The Latin American MERCOSUR bloc[7] is another case of an integration effort where great hope in the beginning only faded away as it was hit by global crisis and negatively impacted by geopolitical power play. Trade between Brazil and Argentina slumped by more than 20% in 2012. Paraguay was temporarily suspended because of internal political conflicts.[8] While Argentina has adopted more protectionist measures, Brazil seems most ready to move ahead with extensive free-trade negotiations with the EU. Accordingly, MERCOSUR is now less prominent, while more attention is paid to the Union of South American Nations (UNASUR)[9] and the newly proposed Pacific Alliance.[10]

ASEAN appears to have made the most progress of all the regional PTAs among countries with comparable levels of development. This is at least the case when measuring levels of intra-regional trade: in ASEAN this accounts for 26% of total trade compared to 15% in MERCOSUR. But it has taken the ten ASEAN members[11] a few decades of inching forward with an ASEAN Free Trade Area (AFTA), even though that still has a substantial exclusion list. ASEAN is nevertheless prepared to move up a gear as it looks forward to the start-up in 2015 of the ASEAN Economic Community (AEC) and further negotiations towards a wider Regional Comprehensive Economic Partnership (RCEP). The AEC is an extensive undertaking that encompasses agreements on investment, trade in services, financial integration (the Chiang Mai Initiative), labour mobility, joint infrastructure investment plus special and differential treatment for Cambodia, Laos and Myanmar. The proposed RCEP would bring together ASEAN and the six countries with which it already has free-trade agreements: China, Japan,

Korea, India, Australia and New Zealand. This more ambitious project may get bogged down by internal geopolitical issues or by external geopolitical diversion in the guise of the TPP, which includes six proposed RCEP members.

With 21 members including the US, China, Russia, Japan and ASEAN, the Asia-Pacific Economic Cooperation (APEC) grouping should count as one of the most serious attempts at cooperation short of creating a fully fledged free-trade area. APEC enjoys the support of national leaders, with an annual summit that provides memorable photos and some networking opportunities. However, there has been little progress towards the main 'Bogor Goals' (agreed at the APEC meeting in Bogor, Indonesia in 1994) to reach an extensive dismantling of trade and investment constraints for the developed members by 2010 and for the developing members by 2020. A mid-term assessment found that the group still had some way to go to achieve free and open trade in the region.[12] Nevertheless APEC has proven to be a vocal cheerleader for the WTO process and has occasionally generated efforts conducive to further work, including the APEC-initiated plurilateral WTO agreement on financial services and the commitment to seriously tackle tariff reduction for environmental goods, expressed in the 2011 Honolulu and 2012 Vladivostok declarations.[13]

One can also point to numerous groupings in Africa to show that traditional regionalism has failed to produce any meaningful integration or developmental benefits to member countries. The long and winding negotiations towards an economic partnership agreement between the EU and the African, Caribbean and Pacific Group of States was meant to promote strong integration in Africa. Instead, it led to acrimonious negotiations that may further drive a wedge between countries on the continent. Meanwhile, the African Union has agreed to move towards a merger of all regional groupings to ultimately establish a

Pan-African Partnership. This process has already started with the formation of a tripartite free-trade area between the East African Community (EAC), the Common Market for Eastern and Southern Africa (COMESA) and the Southern African Development Community (SADC), in which the parties are harmonising and simplifying their rules and regulations to form a core for further integration across Africa.[14]

The opportunity in developmental regionalism

In recent years the role of international trade as a means for inclusive development has been diluted as new, more urgent strategic paradigms have emerged. Governments' commitment to maintaining the openness of their economies has been impacted by domestic fiscal-policy requirements, such as the need for countries to balance their growth strategies between the promotion of export competitiveness and the nurturing of domestic industry; the need to fund development expenditures at home; and the need to support domestic economic growth and employment, especially after the devastating impact of the financial crisis on global trade.

There is public disenchantment with trade liberalisation in industrialised economies, where many believe that trade liberalisation and outsourcing have been responsible for job losses and the suppression of wages. A proper understanding of the link between trade and development must take into account the impact of international production and global supply chains, which have rendered conventional trade statistics and balance-of-trade data less reliable as a measure of competitiveness. New methods of calculating value addition in manufacturing with cross-border trade have shown that the real trade balance, avoiding the duplicate counting of intermediate goods, may have to be adjusted downwards by a factor of 30%. In other words, bilateral trade imbalances may not be as high as imagined.

There is also the growing use of investment measures that restrict trade in the name of social and environmental concerns. These are like non-tariff barriers. A more recent challenge is the rising cost of trade financing, due to Basel III norms[15] being adopted by banks. The European banking system may take some more time cleaning up balance sheets and recapitalising.

All in all, even as the Doha negotiations fail to link up trade with the development agenda of developing countries, advanced countries are seeking to anchor their own trade strategy more firmly on their development concerns. While industrial economies are concerned with declining wages and the closing of technological gaps, the poorer economies are wondering whether they should begin at the beginning, devising new development strategies at home rather than looking to trade as a route to strategic development.

The WTO process of annual review of aid-for-trade programmes has seemingly taken on a life of its own, setting itself apart from the stalling market-access negotiations. From the viewpoint of the United Nations Conference on Trade and Development (UNCTAD), the process could be strengthened if operated in line with the long-standing UNCTAD practice of supporting trade capacity-building and mapping a harmonised trade policy before making a headlong jump into trade openness. Aid for trade could gain from real increases in funding sources, and by both allowing programmes to be determined and owned by the recipient countries, and permitting UNCTAD to carry out more analytical development auditing work. The revival of industrial policy as supported by UNCTAD and the United Nations Industrial Development Organisation (UNIDO) should help developing economies to rebuild their industrialisation process with the creation of their own policy space. Modern industrial policy does not prescribe indefinite protection and state guidance, but is based on a more mixed system in which the market plays a definite role. State roles could only be more pronounced in linking industries with domestic conditions, labour skill training, technology support and R&D, and promoting domestic industry to move up the value chain.

Trade facilitation – reducing red tape in customs and other border procedures – was the main issue salvaging the WTO Bali Ministerial Conference in 2013, and with good reason. As logistical costs are increasing, sometimes up to more than 10% of trade value, reducing tariffs by a few percentage points is less important than increasing efficiency, transparency and connectivity in logistical networks. The impact on landlocked economies, where trade shipment and transaction costs are frequently higher, could also be enormous.[16]

To serve all of the above-mentioned policies, UNCTAD has recommended deeper integration particularly for neighbouring nations and regions with comparable levels of development. For deeper integration to succeed, participating countries must move together all the way to create closer development-cooperation regimes that extensively cover finance, trade, investment, infrastructure, ecology, human resources and more. For Asia, for example, codes of conduct to warrant more stability in the exchange-rate regime and the establishment of an Asian Monetary Fund could be considered. The RCEP, an example of developmental regionalism with a deeper integration effort, could be put into timely operation.

However, the problem now with 'competing regionalism' is that the future trade agenda may be hijacked by the twenty-first-century mega-trade deals beginning to emerge. These could coerce developing countries to open up prematurely, with dire consequences for domestic policy in socially crucial areas such as intellectual property rights and health care, labour standards, environment and trade. These mega-deals also threaten to set up rules and regulations far beyond those agreed at the WTO level and may therefore dilute the WTO's multilateralism by excluding the majority of the membership from the key rule-making process.

This distraction from developmental regionalism may eventually end up leading the global trade community back to the old days when global trade agendas were determined by a few advanced countries. Trade liberalisation should not be viewed only as an end in itself but also as a means for inclusive development. The clock of regionalism cannot be reversed; by going forward the international community should ensure that regionalism enables the promotion of development as much as it ensures sustained trade liberalisation.

Notes

1   The 1992 Blair House Accord was an agreement between the US and EU to reduce agricultural subsidies to exporters and domestic producers.

2   See for example Joseph E. Stiglitz, *Fair Trade for All: How Trade Can Promote Development* (Oxford University Press, 2005)

3   The 'spaghetti bowl effect' is a term coined by Jagdish Bhagwati, in 'US Trade Policy: The Infatuation with Free Trade Agreements', in Claude Barfield (ed.), *The Dangerous Obsession with Free Trade Areas* (Washington DC: American Enterprise Institute, 1995). Rules of origin are meaningless under the WTO, which applies equal tariffs to all imports from WTO member states. However, they operate with FTAs and RTAs that seek to reduce or eliminate tariffs only on particular imports from specific countries. This can work against the formation of the most economically efficient production network.

4   See http://www.statista.com/statistics/268830/unemployment-rate-in-eu-countries/; and http://www.statista.com/statistics/266228/youth-unemployment-rate-in-eu-countries/.

5   Mark Weisbrot, Stephan Lefebvre, and Joseph Sammut, 'Did NAFTA Help Mexico? An Assessment After 20 Years', Center for Economic and Policy Research, Washington DC, 2013.

6   See the World Bank's World Development Indicators, http://data.worldbank.org/country/mexico.

7   MERCOSUR consists of five full members, five associate members and two observer countries. Argentina, Brazil, Paraguay, Uruguay and Venezuela are full members. Bolivia, Chile, Colombia, Ecuador and Peru are associate

members. New Zealand and Mexico have observer status.

8   Paraguay was suspended after it impeached President Fernando Lugo in June 2012, in what regional powers described as a parliamentary coup. Its membership was reinstated after a subsequent presidential election in April 2013.

9   Twelve-member UNASUR brings together the five full-time MERCOSUR members – Argentina, Brazil, Paraguay, Uruguay and Venezuela – with the four full-time members of the Andean Community of Nations (CAN) – Bolivia, Colombia, Ecuador and Peru – with Chile, Guyana and Suriname. Modelled after the EU as a forum for political interaction and interregional trade promotion, its collective GDP exceeds US$4 trillion.

10 The Pacific Alliance has its genesis in the 2011 Lima Declaration, in which Peru, Chile, Colombia and Mexico agreed to form a free-trade region focused on Asia, and to take other steps towards economic integration including facilitating visa-free travel and establishing a common stock exchange. In February 2014, the four countries signed an agreement to eliminate tariffs on 92% of commerce between them. Costa Rica has taken steps towards full membership. For more, see 'Pacific Alliance trade bloc eyes global role', *Strategic Comments*, IISS, 8 April 2014.

11 The ten members of ASEAN are Brunei, Cambodia, Indonesia, Laos, Malaysia, Myanmar (Burma), the Philippines, Singapore, Thailand and Vietnam.

12 Asia-Pacific Economic Cooperation Policy Support Unit, *APEC's Bogor Goals Progress Report*, APEC, Singapore, August 2012.

13 The *Honolulu Declaration – Toward a Seamless Regional Economy*, 19th APEC Leaders' Declaration, Honolulu, US, 12–13 November 2011 was followed by a list of 54 environmental goods attached to the *Vladivostok Declaration – Integrate to Grow, Innovate to Prosper*, 20th APEC Leaders' Declaration, Vladivostok, Russia, 8–9 September 2012. In 2014, the WTO launched negotiations for an environmental-goods agreement, building on the list drawn up in Vladivostok; see WTO, 'Azevêdo welcomes launch of plurilateral environmental goods negotiations', WTO 2014 News Items, 8 July 2014.

14 Begun in 2005, the 'Tripartite' aims to help the African Union (AU) goals of accelerating the economic integration of the continent and achieving sustainable economic development. Encompassing a population of more than 527 million and with a GDP of some US$624 billion, the Tripartite's 26 member states account for 57%–58% of the AU's population and GDP.

15 The cost of borrowing increased after the (voluntary) set of Basel III reforms tightened lending rules, among many other things; see Basel Committee on Banking Supervision, 'International regulatory framework for banks (Basel III)', (Basel, Switzerland: Bank for International Settlements, 2011 and 2013).

16 Ensuring that countries do not apply their technical regulations

and standards to goods in transit is another way of ensuring cost savings for producers in landlocked countries.

CHAPTER FIVE

The geopolitics of the TTIP and the TPP

Ashley J. Tellis

The principal strategic challenge facing the US today is preserving its global primacy in the face of rising challengers such as China. Managing the problems posed by major rivals is nothing new for the US; since the nation's founding, Washington has confronted a series of rivals, first along its land and ocean frontiers, then within its hemisphere and in Asia, and finally in the Old World. Ever since the US emerged as a global power in the aftermath of the Civil War, Washington has assiduously pursued a grand strategy centred not merely on hemispheric control, but also on preventing the Eurasian space from being dominated by any single power, which could both deny the US access to this critical region and enable a rival to eventually challenge the US itself. For this reason, the US confronted Wilhelmine Germany, Nazi Germany, Imperial Japan and finally the Soviet Union to neutralise the threats each posed to American security and American primacy in the international system.

The possibility that China could emerge as the newest rival to the US in Asia and beyond only reinforces the importance of keeping the Eurasian landmass free from hegemonic domination. To be sure, China is still far from being able to realise such an ambition. Beijing confronts an array of serious domestic problems that could prove hard to overcome, and China is surrounded by regional powers who display no interest in subordination. And, of course, China continuously emphasises its desire for a peaceful strategic environment, which includes a disinterest in threatening either its neighbours or the US.

Yet the likelihood of strategic rivalry between Beijing and Washington is high. Sustained economic growth rates have made China the most likely competitor capable of dominating at least the Asian segment of the Eurasian space. As China's growing power spawns expanded interests, these are likely to scrape against the existing security order, whose guarantees are founded upon American primacy. Beijing's quest to recover its pre-colonial political centrality in Asia and its determination to undo the 'century of national humiliation' only intensify the chances of antagonism. Whether Beijing intends it or not, therefore, China's growing strength will position it as a strategic adversary of the US, a prospect made even more consequential given the importance of the Indo-Pacific region as a motor for future global growth.[1]

Since China's continued economic expansion and military modernisation are likely to remain the most important factors disturbing the regional and global security balance, coping with the rise of Chinese power is likely to become the single most significant geopolitical challenge facing the US since its confrontation with the Soviet Union. Washington cannot afford to take lightly the risks accompanying a Chinese eclipse of its status as the premier global power and the resulting constrictions on American strategic autonomy. Since 1945, the US has used its pre-eminent power to structure a rules-based global order based on American preferences, which has enabled a tremendous increase in the wealth and standard of living of its citizens and of individuals around the world. Because Beijing cannot be counted on to maintain this system, much less enhance it, Washington must now adopt a corrective strategy designed to attenuate the risks of China's continued rise.[2]

China's ascendency is unlike previous challenges that Washington has confronted since the early twentieth century. Its distending capabilities have resulted not simply from an internal economic transformation, but rather from the United States' conscious integration of China into the international economic order. This integration, which began under President Jimmy Carter, reached its apotheosis during the presidency of Bill Clinton, when the US – despite significant internal reservations – supported China's membership of the World Trade Organisation (WTO).

This entry into the WTO in 2001 largely formalised Beijing's integration into the global market that the US had steadily nurtured and expanded in the aftermath of the Second World War, principally for the purpose of strengthening the economies of the free world to cope with the threat of global communism. This liberal trading regime, which survived the early abortion of the International Trade Organisation (ITO),[3] gradually grew in strength through the unexpected success of the General Agreement on Tariffs and Trade (GATT). GATT was an American-led enterprise that sought an orderly, reciprocal and multilateral reduction in tariffs, and it provided the foundations upon which a liberal international economic order, despite numerous imperfections, could gradually grow.[4] This multilateral trading system, centred on an asymmetrically open American economy combined with US aid to its war-torn allies in Europe and Asia, stimulated the recovery of these American partners and made them formidable power centres within a few decades. The resultant relative decline of the US was deemed tolerable mainly because it strengthened Washington's alliance relative to the Soviet Union's, a strategy that was handsomely rewarded when the Cold War ended in the peaceful collapse of Soviet power and the recovery of freedom for its satellite states in Eastern Europe.

Flush with this latest geopolitical victory and the resurgence of the liberal vision of peace through interdependence, Washington egged on the international community to create the new WTO in 1995 as the long-sought successor to the ITO. Five years later, the Clinton administration would extend to China permanent normal trade relations, paving the way for its full accession to the WTO. This willingness to integrate China – a nation with no diplomatic relations with the US little more than two decades prior – into the open trading order was viewed as the culmination of the rapprochement with Beijing that had begun in 1971 to tighten the containment of the Soviet Union.

With Moscow's demise as a rival and the US now standing triumphant and alone, aiding China's economic growth in the aftermath of the Cold War by offering it opportunities for expanded trade seemed like a low-risk proposition. Liberals in the US viewed China's integration into the WTO system as a boost for interdependence, which in turn promised greater welfare and peace, although realists were more ambivalent. All viewed China as largely an underdeveloped state, whose integration into the global trading system offered opportunities to improve US gains from trade while providing Beijing with the chance to grow more speedily. However, few policymakers, if any, expected China to grow rapidly enough to become a plausible rival to the US for global power in the new century.

Yet precisely this contingency has now come to pass. While China is, across all dimensions of national power, far from being a genuine peer competitor of the US, there is no other state in the international system that currently possesses as many attributes of a natural rival as China does. Worse, Beijing's military rivalry with the US and its Asian allies has propelled a formidable military-modernisation programme aimed at denying the US its traditional freedom of action along the Asian littorals.[5] The crowning irony, however, is that China has not risen to such levels of pre-eminence simply because of its vast latent capacities. Rather, it was Washington's decisions and policy choices since 1979, and including the immediate post-Cold War period, that midwifed China's growth as a major economic power and as a geopolitical rival of singular danger to the US.

China's integration into the multilateral trading order and its progressive entrenchment as a manufacturing and exporting hub has now tied it to the US and its regional allies in Asia, ensuring for the first time in American history that Washington is economically trapped in a mutual-hostage relationship with its most serious rival. The intense 'global codependency'[6] that defines US–China ties also characterises China's relations with all of its major Asian neighbours, many of whom are treaty allies of the US. This unprecedented condition thus creates the peculiar paradox where China and all of its trading partners are bound ever more deeply through their economic gains, even as they are driven further apart by their national rivalries and Beijing's expanding military power.[7]

Thanks to elevated relative gains, produced by both its comparative advantages as well as its statist policies and controversial trade practices, China has experienced meteoric growth rates that have made it the world's second-largest economy and positioned it to one day possibly overtake the gross national product of the US. Such performance has also enabled China to sustain a defence budget that will rival Washington's within another decade, while already permitting it to levy serious threats on forward-based and forward-operating American forces in and near Asia.[8] If these trends continue, even despite the expected slowing of the Chinese economy, a peculiar power transition is possible in the future. Because this prospect poses a serious threat to the American-led international system, Washington has little choice but to take China's rise more seriously than it ever has.

Responding to a rising China

While the US has successfully confronted rivals before, it has never faced a challenge of the likes posed by China: a political antagonist committed to ending American unipolarity while remaining deeply integrated in a tight trading partnership with Washington and its allies. This competing dualism in US–China relations implies that Washington will succeed only if it pursues subtle and sophisticated approaches, rather than the conceptually simple, though practically burdensome, strategies of the past. If preventative or pre-emptive war is ruled out – as it must be – for prudential and moral reasons today, there are four possible grand strategies available to the US as it prepares to cope with China's rise.

The first grand strategy might be labelled simply, 'Leave Well Alone'. This approach would be based on the premise that China's rise is a natural phenomenon in international history. After all, China has all the attributes that make it a potential great power, and given the historic decisions made by Deng Xiaoping in regard to liberalising the Chinese economy and Bill Clinton's own choice to finally complete Beijing's integration into the international market, China's rise should be treated as the welcome and positive evolution of a country that was long divided and weakened as a result of both foreign occupation and internal fissures. China's high economic growth has already produced remarkable benefits: it has raised millions of ordinary Chinese out of poverty within a generation and China's emergence as a hub for high-quality, low-cost manufacturing has resulted in welfare gains for still more millions of consumers worldwide.

Even China's military modernisation in this context is a natural consequence of China's economic emergence. The historical record suggests that all major states enjoy growth in military expenditure after their economic take-off because their increased wealth creates greater assets to be protected.[9] This expansion in defence spending may exacerbate the security dilemmas with China's neighbours, but these tensions should be mitigated through diplomacy because increased military expenditures do not per se connote threatening expansionist policies. More to the point, all affected states should recognise that military conflicts are not worth the candle in an era of interdependence; they could threaten the growth that benefits all.

The US in particular should be proud of the fact that it has created the conditions that have permitted China's rise. It is a tribute to the US as a hegemonic power, insofar as its creation of global public goods has led to the uplift of an entire nation – in fact the entire Asia-Pacific Rim. China's growing power, accordingly, should be welcomed, not greeted with suspicion. Even though Chinese growth may provoke anxieties in the US and beyond, any overreaction should be discouraged because a growing China is unlikely to disturb the international system.

Since China has expanded principally through international integration, it is likely to uphold the rules that make for good behaviour, because its continued prosperity depends on the continuation of a well-ordered trading system. Consequently, China will subsist as a well-mannered state even if it succeeds the US as a global hegemon; and that prospect should not appear particularly unnerving – and should certainly not provoke destabilising reactions such as containment – because China's interests will demand that it accept and play by the inherited rules.

Leaving a growing China alone, therefore, is good for everybody. If anything, the international community led by the US should aim to integrate China even more tightly into all international institutions and regimes. Even if that ends up stimulating greater Chinese growth, the increased stakes that China will have in a peaceful international community will prevent it from using its increased power irresponsibly, because of the dangers of destroying the very integration that has made its success possible.

Although this liberal vision of integrating China peacefully is undoubtedly attractive, it has limitations. The chief weakness in this regard is that it presumes a certain pre-existing harmony of interests, such that even China's pursuit of parochial interests will not disturb the international equilibrium. Moreover, it assumes that China's dependence on international integration will always prevent it from pursuing policies that may undermine the interests of other states, given that the mutual search for absolute gains would be at risk if it did.

The history of international relations, however, does not support such optimism and the transition period from British to American hegemony confirms this point abundantly. Even though Great Britain and the US shared common values and even common adversaries, Washington pursued its interests in the early post-war period in a way that fundamentally undermined British objectives.[10] Similarly, China could well uphold the scaffolding of the institutional arrangements it inherits from the US but fundamentally transform their manner of functioning, and their specific aims, to Washington's continuing detriment. Consequently, the policy of leaving well alone – or persistent integration *simpliciter* – is unlikely to serve US interests in the manner imagined by its advocates.

Given that the policy of letting China be fails to immunise the US against the risks that Beijing could use the growing, and disproportionate, benefits of interdependence to advance its own interests at American expense, even if only peacefully, Washington could pursue a second strategy that might be labelled, 'Let's Make a Deal'. The key characteristic of this second grand strategy would be that, instead of relying on China to uphold the inherited order mainly out of self-interest, the US would tacitly or explicitly negotiate a Chinese agreement to preserve that order in continuing collaboration with Washington.

Negotiating such a pact while China is still some distance away from genuine parity with the US – a concept sometimes colloquially referred to as G2[11] – has the advantage of 'socialising' Beijing into accepting the legitimacy of the US-created international system before it fulfils its great-power potential. Since it is not yet invested in protecting this order, giving it the rights and privileges of management a little before it inherits these powers naturally through continuing economic growth could secure its allegiance to upholding that order long before it might be tempted to revise it.

Making a bilateral deal with China, thus, has a certain attractiveness. For China, entering into duopolistic management of the international system with the US when it is on the cusp of becoming a genuine peer would provide it with important legitimisation benefits vis-à-vis the international community and ease the path to leadership status. For the US, it would offer the advantage of avoiding a costly and possibly unnecessary rivalry with China, at the same time as securing Chinese political and economic resources to uphold a system that, while beneficial to all, is increasingly costly for Washington to maintain unilaterally. More importantly, giving Beijing a joint management role through an increased presence in international institutions, a privileged position in global rule-making and possibly a division of labour in providing global public goods, ensures that if a succession occurs in the global system, the American legacy of a liberal institutional order will be protected by a rising China. It will have had a significant stake in maintaining that order up to that point.[12]

For all its benefits, however, the strategy of duopolistic management of the international order has dangerous downsides for the US. For starters, the idea of cooperation between China and the US may simply not survive if American power continues to weaken in relative terms. In other words, the gains of the G2 system could vanish to American disadvantage if the duopoly becomes increasingly lopsided as a result of accumulating Chinese power. Even the possibility of such an outcome should deter the US from embarking on any duopolistic arrangements prematurely; in fact, it may be in Washington's interests to hold out until China becomes a genuine peer and then, depending on its behaviour at that point, make the decision about engaging China in managing the international system while recognising that such a deal might not survive a longer-term shift in the two states' relative power.

Most problematic of all, however, is the fact that a duopolistic approach to managing international politics would run afoul of the interests of many other Asian and European partners of the US: many of the former – especially Japan and India – have little interest in being subordinated to a hegemonic China in Asia or in becoming secondary players in a Sino-American managed global order. Consequently, any efforts by Washington to construct such a duopoly would rend asunder the Asian geopolitical system, with unpredictable consequences for American and Chinese interests. Thus, whatever its appeal to Chinese policymakers today, a duopolistic approach is far less attractive to the US as a long-term solution.

If neither leaving well alone nor making a deal advances America's interests in preserving its apex power position or protecting the international regime that it sired in the post-war period, China's continued accumulation of power – even if at a slower rate – might require the US to consider carefully the third grand strategic option: 'Constrain Chinese Success'. Whether implemented in its more minimalistic form of simply limiting China's growing capacity to undermine American interests or in its more maximalist version, which requires the US to actively undermine China's rise, exercising this grand strategic option would in effect be a Machiavellian solution to 'seeing inconveniences from afar'. Throughout the Cold War, depending on circumstances, Washington toggled between both types of containment strategy against the Soviet Union, although it was clear since its articulation in NSC-68[13] that the US sought to ultimately undermine its communist adversary through all means short of war.

In any event, a strategy of constraining Chinese success through containment would require Washington to limit China's connectivity with the major economic centres of power globally, ensuring that these entities were tied only to the US, its allies and one another – as was the case during the Cold War. The US would also have to integrate all Asian states feeling threatened by China into either a unified geopolitical alliance system or into even tighter bilateral security arrangements primarily focused on arresting Beijing's expanding power. In addition, Washington would need to develop collective defence strategies through common military institutions or coordinated defence arrangements that prescribed how the combat capabilities available to the US and its partners would be used to defeat Chinese aggression or ability to exercise coercive power. Finally, the US would have to pursue a larger ideological campaign worldwide aimed at delegitimising the Chinese state and government, as well as inflaming internal Chinese tensions over Tibet, Xinjiang and Taiwan.[14]

A purposeful strategy of containment along these lines would limit China's capacity to threaten American power; in fact, it would prevent China from even catching up to the US. If Machiavelli were around, a strategy of containment in this form would incur his enthusiastic approbation because it would undermine China's ability to evolve to the point where it could ever become a peer competitor of the US, thereby protecting America's position as the hegemonic power in international politics for a long time to come. However, the US is currently unlikely to embark on such a policy because it still holds on to the belief – nurtured by its liberal inheritance – that China is not inevitably destined to become an adversary, and that so long as the possibility of an amiable relationship persists Washington should do all in its power to prevent an open-ended rivalry from developing.

Other, more material, considerations are germane: even if the containment of China were desirable on the grounds that all classical realists would prefer, there is presently no way to constrain Chinese economic growth by eliminating the one critical factor that has made all the difference to its success: its access to international markets. Because the US made the fateful decision to integrate China into the liberal international order as far back as 1979 – a policy direction faithfully followed by every US administration since Jimmy Carter's and only brought to its apotheosis by Bill Clinton's decision to support Beijing's entry into the multilateral trading system in 2001 – both Washington and its allies are now trapped in a situation where all parties, including China, are dependent on mutual trading relations for their growth and welfare. In such circumstances, no matter how threatening China may one day become to their geopolitical interests, China's trading partners have no incentive to cut commercial ties with Beijing because of the absolute gains they would sacrifice as a result. This problem of mutual interdependence did not exist during the Cold War, making the strategy of containment vis-à-vis the Soviet Union possible.[15]

Given the web of economic ties that bind China and the larger international community today, the strategy of containment is simply unavailable to Washington today. Even more problematically, it is likely to remain beyond American reach precisely because of the success of the post-war US-led international order: unless China transmutes itself into an avaricious threat to global or regional security writ large, it is doubtful that Beijing's trading partners will forego the absolute gains deriving from trade with China just to curb the political ascendancy that is fundamentally fuelled by its integration into the global economy.

As a consequence, China's partners may find themselves in a situation where it is too late to correct the evolving imbalances of power, either regionally or globally, because they cannot resolve the conflicts between absolute and relative gains in any decisive way. Admittedly, this makes them vulnerable to Chinese strategies of 'salami-slicing', where China exploits its superior gains from trade to amass enough political power to permit it to extract successive small concessions, which steadily strengthens its own pre-eminence while avoiding any startling aggression that causes its partners to curtail the trade links that fuel Beijing's continued rise. However, China's partners will likely seek to manage these challenges through internal and external balancing that does *not* put at risk their commercial ties with China.

The only alternative that stands a chance of success in these circumstances is the fourth grand strategy which might be labeled, 'Let's Run Faster'. Such a grand strategy, unlike the central idea enshrined in containment, does not focus on constricting China's ascendancy either by cutting it off from the global economy or limiting its power by diverting its state capacity to deal with internal crises stimulated from abroad. Instead, the strategy of running faster than China hinges on the idea that the existing international regime should be preserved because, although it fuels Beijing's expanding power, it also provides gains for China's partners.

Since these gains currently accrue disproportionately to China, however, this fourth approach seeks to neutralise these asymmetric advantages through a multi-pronged strategy that includes: improving the efficiency and the innovative capacity of the American economy to enable the US to dominate the new leading sectors of the global economy; renewing the ability of the US to project its military power globally despite all anticipated opposition; buttressing the national power of the countries geopolitically pivotal for balancing China – Japan, India, Indonesia, Australia, Vietnam and Singapore, among others – so as to amplify the constraints on Beijing's capacity to misuse its power and provide Washington with a local first line of defence; and, finally, to erect a new institutional overlay on the multilateral trading system that would enable the US and its friends to correct the losses suffered from China's imperfect entry into the liberal trading order while at the same time enhancing their own gains from trade. This last strategy would permit the US to both stay competitive in any upcoming rivalry for hegemony with China and enable it to continue bearing the supernormal costs required to provide those global public goods essential for the success of the liberal international order.[16]

The advantage of such a grand strategy is that it requires neither the dismantling of the open global order simply because it has fuelled the rise of new competitors, nor the undertaking of focused measures to limit the growth of those competitors, such as China. Given that international politics will remain largely a competitive system, the strategy of running faster than China instead has the advantage of increasing the specific gains accruing to the US and its friends, while still preserving the larger liberal order that has served the interests of all.

It is in this context that the strategy of pursuing less-than-universal trading agreements such as the Transatlantic Trade and Investment Partnership (TTIP) and the Trans-Pacific Partnership (TPP) must be considered.[17] Neither agreement is intended to substitute for the current multilateral regime. The efforts to expand the latter will continue apace, but these will be supplemented by a superstructure of bilateral and regional trade agreements (RTAs) that are intended not to contain China – in the specific sense defined earlier – but rather to enable the US and its partners to stay ahead of China in coming years. Achieving this is critical for the survival of the liberal international order inaugurated by America in the post-war period. If American power weakens irretrievably, it is likely that the current international regime, which has served many common interests beyond unique American objectives, could either decay to the disadvantage of all or be replaced by some other Sino-centric alternative that is less beneficial to the US specifically and to many others generally.

The logic of RTAs in enhancing US power

Any grand strategy that seeks to protect American hegemony in an economically interdependent environment must focus on how expanding global trade strengthens the material foundations of US power. Enlarging the international trading regime and increasing civilian trade must simultaneously yield enhanced absolute gains and improved relative gains for the US, irrespective of the tensions between these objectives.

Deepening interdependence allows all trade partners to further specialise in accordance with their comparative advantages, thereby increasing their growth rates. The history of the post-war period suggests that expanding trade remains perhaps the most effective external instrument for building comprehensive national power. Tighter international trade links might also serve American strategic interests, as integrating China into the trading order would force Beijing to realise that its growing power is better served by internal development and robust external markets than by military alternatives. Moreover, enlarging the current trading system to include major developing countries – many of which were once peripheral to international trade – will increase the United States' absolute gains insofar as it reduces tariffs and non-tariff barriers and accesses relatively high-growth markets.

The most effective means for achieving this end is through a further expansion of the multilateral trading system under the auspices of the WTO, but it is unlikely that this by itself will yield the absolute gains necessary for the United States' emerging competition with China. Pessimism on this count is justified, not merely because of the cumbersome processes of securing consensus within the WTO, but, more fundamentally, because the huge divide in development levels between the rich and poor states makes it virtually impossible for them to arrive at a mutually advantageous bargain on trade liberalisation that is both wide and deep. Nothing short of that outcome is required if the US is to bet on the global multilateral trading regime to successfully manage the rise of China.

Even if Washington manages to secure some progress in these circumstances, any victory for the US in the WTO will likely imply only a low-common-denominator advance in expanding global trade. Such gains could actually yield bigger advantages for Beijing because, among other reasons, China's trade-to-GDP ratio is almost double that of the US, and China's trade still consists primarily of merchandise exports rather than the high-end services associated with the US, which are more likely to escape WTO expansion.

Consequently, American policymakers today should focus as much on securing increased relative gains for the US as on expanding absolute benefits. The best way to secure these dividends is to invest heavily in concluding bilateral or regional trade agreements (RTAs) with America's friends and allies, especially those states lying along China's immediate and extended periphery; these are ties that Washington seeks to strengthen anyway for its larger geopolitical purposes. Such accords would be mutually beneficial in multiple ways: the regional partners would have enhanced access to the huge American market for their products while at the same time availing themselves of US capital, high-value-added services and high-technology goods. This would raise growth rates in both directions through arrangements that incidentally, and at least for now, have the advantage of excluding China. RTAs, such as the TTIP and the TPP, that incorporate this specific benefit might be even more valuable to Washington because, to the degree that they genuinely reduce non-tariff and behind-the-border trade barriers, they offer heightened relative gains to the US and its allies.

Washington, accordingly, ought to concentrate on concluding these two agreements, along with other efforts to strengthen North American (or American hemispheric) trading. The TTIP is clearly the most important geopolitically, because the US and the Atlantic community represent the two biggest concentrations of economic power internationally. As Daniel Hamilton and Joseph Quinlan have summarised it: 'There is no commercial artery in the world as large as the one binding the US and Europe together. The transatlantic economy still accounts for over 50% of world GDP in terms of value and 41% in terms of purchasing power, is the largest and wealthiest market in the world, is at the forefront of global R&D, and drives global foreign direct investment and global mergers and acquisitions activity.'[18]

Several studies have indicated that the conclusion of a comprehensive transatlantic trade pact would boost overall trade between the US and EU by as much as 50%, at a value of over US$200 billion annually, and increase annual growth rates in the EU and US by roughly 0.9 and 0.8 percentage points, respectively. Such performance, moreover, would stimulate global incomes, leading to an increase of some US$140bn annually.[19] Eliminating current impediments to trade and quickly completing the negotiations 'on one tank of gas', as US Trade Representative Michael Froman put it, should accordingly be an American priority.[20]

Beyond all the economic advantages of the TTIP lie the hard realities of power politics. Most of the European states involved are among America's strongest allies, thus making the task of 'turning the world's premier security alliance into the world's premier economic pact' particularly important.[21] More robust economic integration between these states would increase absolute gains for all parties without creating any of the corrosive problems stemming from disparities in relative gains in trade between competitors, all the while elevating relative gains for Washington vis-à-vis China. These benefits might also consolidate the economic and technological power of the West and the US for at least another generation, if not longer.

A speedy conclusion of the TTIP would also serve as a cudgel for Washington to use in the other difficult negotiations associated with the TPP. A successful TTIP would reduce mostly non-tariff barriers, so Asian states, unlikely to accept weaker Pacific economic integration than their Atlantic peers, could be spurred into addressing both tariff and non-tariff obstacles.

Successfully negotiating the TPP is important because the Asia-Pacific region is already vital to the US economy, absorbing 60% of its exported goods, 72% of its agricultural products and 39% of its private services in 2011.[22] In 2013, Pacific Rim countries supplied almost 34% of American imports and absorbed nearly 25% of its exports.[23] The complexity of negotiating a high-quality trade agreement with 11 countries with diverse levels of development and widely variable tariff and non-tariff barriers cannot be overestimated. However, the economic growth and strategic importance of the countries involved in the TPP make bringing a trans-Pacific trade pact to completion a necessary proposition.

Many TPP partners still possess relatively protected economies, so the biggest gains to the US would derive from prying open their hitherto closed markets. International economists, such as Peter Petri and Michael Plummer, have estimated that a successfully concluded TPP agreement would raise the United States' GDP by 0.4% by 2025.[24] This improvement, while smaller than the estimated gains from a TTIP agreement, is nothing to be scoffed at in a mature economy, especially when relatively underdeveloped competitors like China chalk up much higher rates of economic growth.

Consequently, concluding the TPP speedily is important, all difficulties notwithstanding. In fact, given US strategic objectives in Asia and the necessity of strengthening the power of states located along China's periphery, Washington should aim to eventually include India in the TPP as well. Admitting New Delhi into the negotiations would benefit the states involved because of the size of India's domestic market and its growth strategy, which favours domestic consumption. It would also be a profitable move for New Delhi, since such a trading arrangement would compel it to accelerate its domestic economic reforms while also increasing its national power.

Unsurprisingly, Indian policymakers, amid fears of a weakening multilateral trade system, have recently expressed interest in exploring membership of the TPP.

These two mega-RTAs thus hold out the promise of increasing US gains from trade and elevating the overall growth rate of the US and its friends. To the degree that these agreements fulfil this potential, they will help buttress American hegemony, in effect amplifying the pay-offs from (hopefully) prudent domestic economic decisions. Most importantly, however, because the distribution of benefits presently excludes China, they will provide Washington with improved relative gains vis-à-vis Beijing, the sine qua non for maintaining American primacy in a competitive international system.

Admittedly, as neoclassical economists would correctly argue, such RTAs are less efficient than their universal counterparts for increasing overall growth, because their trade-diversion effects distort the patterns of comparative advantage and they make only some states better off in comparison to not trading.[25] Yet these agreements represent the only alternative at a time when the multilateral trading system is failing to produce the maximum gains from trade possible – due, ironically, to an excess of democracy in the negotiating regime.[26] In a purely economic sense, therefore, it is useful to conceptualise these FTAs as transitional endeavours that would promote liberalisation in order to eventually enlarge the global system of exchange.[27] Whether this vision is ultimately realised or not, RTAs, by debarring competitors or by compelling them to liberalise and end their asymmetric advantages, offer the US a strategic opportunity to elevate its relative gains vis-à-vis China.

The success of this approach, however, will hinge on keeping China out of these regional agreements for as long as possible, or at least until the US can 'buy back' the relative gains it has lost as a result of China's entry into the multilateral trading system. If US policymakers pursue the selective deepening of globalisation as a means of elevating future American growth in this way, they will have to reject any present Chinese overtures about joining agreements such as the TPP. To date, US officials have equivocated. Recently, National Security Advisor Susan Rice blandly stated, 'We welcome any nation that is willing to live up to the high standards of this agreement to join and share in the benefits of the TPP, and that includes China.'[28] While the diplomatic necessity for appearing inclusive is understandable, the strategic necessity for excluding China is overwhelming.

China's own position on this issue is also not yet settled. Beijing initially viewed the TPP with unambiguous anxiety, perceiving it, in Duke University professor Bai Gao's description, as a 'securitisation of trade policy' driven by the intention to contain China.[29] Since then, Chinese attitudes have devolved into schizophrenia, alternately judging the TPP as a thinly veiled instrument of containment or as a beckoning cornucopia. Despite this ambivalence, Beijing now appears to be steadily but quietly gravitating towards the TPP. This is hardly surprising. As one analysis demonstrated, trade diversion would cost China more than US$100bn in lost annual income and exports if it were excluded from the TPP. Moreover, China could be shut out of a group that could ultimately form the basis of an American containment of China.[30]

The gains China would accumulate by joining the TPP are thus obvious, but the risks to Washington of including Beijing as a negotiating partner are also great. To begin with, the diversity of tariff and non-tariff barriers among the negotiating Asia-Pacific nations makes it extremely hard to conclude a truly high-quality agreement. Including China as a negotiating partner, considering its substantial structural protectionism, would likely lead to a 'Swiss cheese' agreement so full of holes as to deny the US the gains that could only arise from a genuinely ambitious trade accord.

Given this danger, Washington should keep China out of all TPP negotiations until an exemplary pact is negotiated. Irrespective of what China does at that point, the US will come out ahead. If China declines to participate on the grounds that it cannot acquiesce to an agreement that it was not involved in negotiating, Washington would still enjoy enhanced relative gains vis-à-vis Beijing because it would continue to profit from increased commerce with its closed set of friends. If China chooses to join a high-quality TPP that was concluded in its absence, Washington would likely obtain even greater relative gains, given that the trade liberalisation necessary for China to join the agreement would eliminate all of Beijing's current asymmetrical advantages while giving the US enhanced access to a large market. In any event, the US can continue to pursue exclusive trade policies without apology, since China has sought similar arrangements such as the China–Japan–South Korea agreement and the Regional Comprehensive Economic Partnership (RCEP).[31]

While there is no need for US policymakers to advertise any reluctance to admit China into TPP negotiations, they should certainly desist from welcoming its participation until a final agreement is reached. Most importantly, they ought to at least be clear in their own minds about why strategic logic demands Beijing's current exclusion from these negotiations.

Conclusion

Although the US has championed free-trade universalism since its founding, its commitment to free trade was always subordinated to politics. For most of American history, Washington's approach to international trade was formed by internal politics influenced by business cycles, interest groups, regional divides and shifting party positions.[32] In the aftermath of the Second World War, the US once again launched an effort to construct a global economic order based on free-trade universalism, but settled for a more circumscribed system of managed free trade, centred on reciprocity.

This limited framework served the US well during the Cold War. It enabled the alliance partners to rapidly resuscitate themselves, while simultaneously permitting the Western coalition to enjoy substantial gains from trade relative to its adversaries. These benefits supplemented the enormous internal productivity of the American economy, which in turn produced the superior economic growth that enabled the US to outrun the Soviet Union and provoke its collapse. The American triumph in the Cold War led to a further expansion of the global trading order to finally formally include China, despite Beijing's continued pursuit of statist policies. As a result of the disproportionate gains from imbalanced trade that ensued, China's growth has been even more meteoric than it might otherwise have been. What is most unsettling, however, is that Beijing has used its gains from trade to rapidly modernise its military forces, and to begin to threaten most of its major regional trading partners as well as the guardian of the larger international order, the US itself.

While China's economic strategy of international integration is thus increasingly at odds with its geopolitical strategy of increasing its coercive capabilities directed against its major trading partners, Washington's own post-Cold War strategy is also afflicted by the awkward contradiction of sustaining an international economic regime that produces great benefits for the US and others while simultaneously fuelling the growth of what could be its most significant rival. Three of the four possible grand strategies aimed at mitigating this dilemma –

leaving China alone, making a duopolistic deal with Beijing and constraining Chinese success – all fail to limit the dangers posed by a rising China to the US and its friends.

Only the fourth strategy, centred not on inhibiting China's growth but on improving America's strategic performance, cuts the Gordian knot to enable the US to protect its global hegemony while continuing China's integration into the liberal international order. The policy of incorporating RTAs into the existing multilateral trading system accordingly provides Washington with the opportunity to secure both increased absolute gains and increased relative gains vis-à-vis China, thereby protecting its international position. The US should not shrink from pursuing such self-interested modifications to the global trading order because, as its own history reveals, American trade policy has always been shaped by political imperatives rather than the dogmas of neoclassical economics. In an era of rising Chinese ascendency, protecting American strategic interests through new mega-RTAs does not constitute a geo-economic containment of China – a losing proposition at its best. Rather, it represents an effort to leapfrog Beijing in the race to success during yet another long cycle in world politics.

Notes

1   See Aaron L. Friedberg, *A Contest for Supremacy: China, America, and the Struggle for Mastery in Asia* (New York: W.W. Norton and Company, 2011); and Dan Blumenthal and Phillip Swagel, *An Awkward Embrace: The United States and China in the 21st Century* (Washington DC: American Enterprise Institute, 2012), pp. 8–11.

2   Ashley J. Tellis, *Balancing without Containment: An American Strategy for Managing China* (Washington DC: Carnegie Endowment for International Peace, 2014), pp. 11–15.

3   The ITO was created by the Havana Charter signed in March 1948, but faded away after this charter was never ratified by the United States Congress.

4   For an excellent overview of the origins of GATT, see Thomas W. Zeiler, *Free Trade, Free World: The*

Advent of GATT (Chapel Hill, NC and London: University of North Carolina Press, 1999).

5   See Ashley J. Tellis and Travis Tanner (eds), *Strategic Asia 2012–13: China's Military Challenge* (Washington DC and Seattle: National Bureau of Asian Research, 2012).

6   Catherine L. Mann, 'Breaking Up is Hard to Do: Global Co-Dependency, Collective Action, and the Challenges of Global Adjustment', *CESifo Forum*, vol. 6, no. 1, Spring 2005, pp. 16–23.

7   Ashley J. Tellis, *Power Shift: How the West Can Adapt and Thrive in an Asian Century* (Washington DC: German Marshall Fund of the United States, 2010), pp. 3–4.

8   Aaron L. Friedberg, *Beyond Air–Sea Battle: The Debate Over US Military Strategy in Asia*, Adelphi Book 444 (Abingdon: Routledge for the IISS, 2014).

9   See Jasen J. Castillo et al., *Military Expenditures and Economic Growth* (Santa Monica, CA: RAND Corporation, 2000).

10 Corelli Barnett, *The Collapse of British Power* (New York: Morrow, 1972), 589ff.

11 Zbigniew Brzezinski, 'Moving Towards a Reconciliation of Civilizations', *China Daily*, 15 January 2009.

12 Hugh White, *The China Choice: Why America Should Share Power* (Collingwood, Australia: Black Inc., 2012).

13 Only declassified in 1975, the 58-page NSC Report No. 68 was one of the most influential US government documents during the Cold War. Its authors argued that the best response to a fundamentally hostile Soviet Union that would soon acquire more nuclear and other weapons was 'a more rapid build-up of political, economic, and military strength and thereby of confidence in the free world … consistent with progress toward achieving our fundamental purpose. The frustration of the Kremlin design requires the free world to develop a successfully functioning political and economic system and a vigorous political offensive against the Soviet Union.' See National Security Council Report No. 68, 'United States Objectives and Programs for National Security', 14 April 1950, http://www.fas.org/irp/offdocs/nsc-hst/nsc-68.htm.

14 Tellis, *Balancing without Containment*, p. 29.

15 Melvyn P. Leffler, 'The Emergence of an American Grand Strategy', in Melvyn P. Leffler and Odd Arne Westad (eds), *The Cambridge History of the Cold War: 1* (Cambridge: Cambridge University Press, 2010), pp. 67–73.

16 For a detailed elaboration of this four-pronged strategy, see Tellis, *Balancing without Containment*, pp. 35–84.

17 See Glossary.

18 Daniel S. Hamilton and Joseph P. Quinlan, *The Transatlantic Economy 2013: Annual Survey of Jobs, Trade and Investment Between the United States and Europe* (Washington DC: Center for Transatlantic Relations, 2013), p. 18.

19 See 'Transatlantic trade talks: Opening shots', *The Economist*, 6 July 2013; and Joseph Francois, Miriam Manchin, Hanna Norberg, Olga Pindyuk and Patrick Tomberger,

Reducing Transatlantic Barriers to Trade and Investment: An Economic Assessment, Final Project Report for the European Commission (London: Centre for Economic Policy Research, 2013).

20 Michael Froman, remarks at the Transatlantic Trade and Investment Partnership First Round Opening Plenary, Washington DC, 8 July 2013, www.ustr.gov/about-us/press-office/speeches/transcripts/2013/july/amb-froman-ttip-opening-plenary.

21 Marta Dassù and Charles A. Kupchan, 'Pivot to a Trans-Atlantic Market', *New York Times*, 13 June 2013.

22 'The United States in the Trans-Pacific Partnership: Increasing American Exports, Supporting American Jobs', Office of the US Trade Representative Press Office Fact Sheets, June 2012, https://ustr.gov/about-us/policy-offices/press-office/fact-sheets/2012/june/us-tpp-increasing-american-exports-supporting-american-jobs/.

23 See 'Annual Trade Highlights: 2013 Press Highlights', US Census Bureau, https://www.census.gov/foreign-trade/statistics/highlights/annual.html; and 'Trade in Goods with Pacific Rim', US Census Bureau, https://www.census.gov/foreign-trade/balance/c0014.html.

24 Peter Petri and Michael Plummer, 'The Trans-Pacific Partnership and Asia-Pacific Integration: Policy Implications', Peterson Institute for International Economics, June 2012.

25 Jagdish Bhagwati, *Free Trade Today* (Princeton, NJ: Princeton University Press, 2003), pp. 91–109.

26 Arvind Subramanian, 'Too Much Legitimacy Can Hurt Global Trade', *Financial Times*, 13 January 2013.

27 C. Fred Bergsten, *Competitive Liberalization and Global Free Trade*, Working Paper 96–15 (Washington DC: Peterson Institute for International Economics, 1996).

28 Susan E. Rice, 'America's Future in Asia', remarks at Georgetown University, Washington DC, 21 November 2013, http://www.whitehouse.gov/the-press-office/2013/11/21/remarks-prepared-delivery-national-security-advisor-susan-e-rice.

29 Bai Gao, 'From Maritime Asia to Continental Asia: China's Responses to the Challenge of the Trans-Pacific Partnership', Conference Paper presented at 'The Trans-Pacific Partnership and Taiwan's Future Development Strategy', Stanford, CA, 11 October 2013, http://iis-db.stanford.edu/evnts/7924/Gao.TPP_paper.pdf.

30 I am grateful to Fred Bergsten for sharing this data with me. It derives from Peter A. Petri, Michael Plummer and Fan Zhai, 'The Effects of a China–US Free Trade Agreement', subsequently published in Fred Bergsten and Gary Hufbauer (eds), *Bridging the Pacific: Toward Free Trade and Investment Between China and the United States* (Washington DC: Peterson Institute for International Economics, 2014). The data is based on simulations for the year 2025 on the assumption that the TPP would have 16 members (with Korea, Indonesia, the Philippines and Thailand as the additional four).

31 See Glossary.

32 Douglas A. Irwin, 'Historical Aspects of US Trade Policy',

National Bureau of Economic Research, Summer 2006, http://www.nber.org/reporter/summer06/irwin.html; and Pietro S. Nivola, 'The New Protectionism: US Trade Policy in Historical Perspective', *Political Science Quarterly,* vol. 101, no. 4, 1986, pp. 577–600.

CHAPTER SIX

The evolving geo-economics of world trade

Braz Baracuhy

The map of world trade has been redrawn. New geo-economic forces are interacting with pre-existing geopolitical realities and reshaping the conditions under which the process of economic globalisation takes place. After an initial confluence between geo-economics and geopolitics that defined the power equilibrium of globalisation in the 1990s, the international system is now witnessing the structural mismatch between global geo-economics and geopolitics. The diffusion of economic power is decoupling geo-economics from prevailing geopolitical conditions. Evolving trends in global trade patterns and international trade negotiations display the complexities of a polycentric globalisation.

Economic globalisation has been commonly understood as the process of growing economic integration and interdependence among national economies through flows of commerce and capital.[1] The existing configuration of international power and the underlying balance between geo-economics and geopolitics fundamentally affect that process.

Globalisation requires a favourable international power equilibrium, which provides order, stability, institutions and incentives to the day-to-day operations of international economic relations – from the security of sea lanes for trading goods, inputs and energy to the rules-based structure of the international trade and finance regimes. Kevin O'Rourke is correct to stress that the balance of power has influenced trade throughout history. 'The pattern of trade can only be understood as being the outcome of some military or political equilibrium between contending powers,' he writes.[2]

International trade has effects on the distribution of production, income and wealth, and consequently on the global balance of geo-economic power. Geopolitical power is one of the key factors shaping the strategic environment and the institutional setting within which trade takes place. The dynamic confluence between geo-economics and geopolitics ultimately reinforces the configuration of international power and supports the existing international order. On the connection between international polarity and the evolving economic globalisation, political scientist Kenneth Waltz has observed that: 'The international economy, like national economies, operates within a set of rules and institutions that have to be made and sustained.'[3]

International trade is one of the forces contributing to shifts in the global distribution of economic power and the geo-economic landscape. New geo-economic powers have emerged. The previous alignment between geo-economics and geopolitics that structurally shaped economic globalisation is now shattering. International trade is decoupling from geo-economics. Recent trends and deadlocks in international trade negotiations are symptoms of those transformations.

Mapping the patterns of global trade

The evolving patterns of international trade – its configurations, concentrations, geographic flows and interdependences

– have formed new geo-economic realities in recent decades.

The WTO's *World Trade Report 2013* addressed some of the central factors reshaping international trade relations.[4] International trade has broadly reflected the trend of a global redistribution in geo-economic power, especially from the North Atlantic to Asia and the emerging world. Developing countries' share in world exports increased from 34% in 1980 to 47% in 2011, while developed economies recorded a decline from 66% to 53%. In particular, China's share of world exports rose from 1% to 11% during the same period, while the US, EU, and Japan experienced relative declines in trade exports. Developing countries' share of world imports also increased from 29% in 1980 to 42% in 2011, while developed countries experienced a relative decline from 71% to 58%. China's imports rose from 1% to 10%; and the US, EU, and Japan global import shares declined.

Reflecting these geo-economic structural changes, a geographical redistribution of trade flows has emerged. Shares of south–south trade among developing economies increased to 24% of world trade in 2011, from 8% in 1990 and 16% in 2005, while shares of north–north trade among developed economies declined from 56% in 1990 to 36% in 2011. North–south trade has been relatively stable: 33% in 1990 and 38% in 2011.

Intra-regional trade flows are a central geo-economic feature of recent years. A case in point is Asia, where intra-regional trade shares rose from 47% (US$739 billion) of that region's total trade in 1990 to 52% (US$5.5 trillion) in 2011. In 2011, the EU's intra-regional share of total trade flow was at 71% (US$6.6 trillion) and North America's at 48% (US$2.2 trillion). By contrast, trade flows are predominantly extra-regional in South and Central America (74%), Africa (88%) and the Middle East (85%).[5]

Intra-regional trends in Asia, North America and Europe are partially the result of transnational corporations' global value chains (GVCs) operating in those regions, linking foreign direct investments and trade in goods, intermediate inputs and services, in what trade economist Richard Baldwin has aptly named regional 'factory economies' (e.g., 'Factory Asia', etc.). Firms from 'headquarter economies' (essentially the US, Germany, Japan and, increasingly, Korea) shape supply-chain networks and establish a hub-and-spoke structure with factory economies.[6] GVCs create a specific kind of international trade: supply-chain trade. The United Nations Conference on Trade and Development (UNCTAD) estimates that supply-chain trade (intra-firm and inter-firm related trade) accounts for 80% of global trade. Although supply-chain trade takes place predominantly within 'regional factories', there are complex inter-regional interdependences. The US, China, Germany and Japan are at the heart of supply-chain trade at the global level.[7]

The level of trade interdependence among different regions of the world, and the centrality of Asia in those global trade flows, can be observed from the inter-regional shares of total world trade in 2011, in particular between Asia and Europe (8.8%), and between Asia and North America (7.8%). South and Central America's share of global trade with Asia increased from 0.8% in 1990 to 2.0% in 2011, whereas Latin America's proportionate share of trade with North America and Europe declined. In the same period, Africa's trade share with Asia rose from 0.6% to 1.7%, while its trade-flow share with Europe declined from 3.4% to 2.3% of global trade. Middle East–Asia trade flows increased from 3.2% of global trade in 1990 to 5.1% in 2011.

The world trade landscape has been transformed in the past few decades. Geo-economic trading arcs have taken shape, linking new regional pivots and players. New poles of geo-economic power have emerged. Trade interdependences are increasing, both intra- and inter-regionally. Transnational corporations and global value-chain trade are part of this picture. Geo-economics, economic diplomacy and international business are interacting in new and complex ways.

Balancing geo-economics and geopolitics

Globalisation has undergone a structural shift. Changes in the international power equilibrium are reshaping the conditions under which economic globalisation evolves.

Based on the post-Cold War structural power convergence between geo-economics and geopolitics, globalisation in the 1990s was essentially monocentric. The North Atlantic was the geo-economic centre of the world. Globalisation spread out from that North Atlantic core to encompass the whole world of trade and financial relations. To a large extent, the Group of Seven (G7) leading industrial nations – the US, Britain, Canada, France, Germany, Italy and Japan – lay at the heart of this global geo-economic system. In the early 1990s, the G7 generated 55% of world output and was responsible for 53% of global exports. To be sure, within the G7, the hegemonic role of the US in building and sustaining this geo-economic structure of growth, production, trade, investment, innovation and institutions cannot be underestimated. The US functioned as the dynamic hub of the global economy, linking with Western Europe and Japan as economic partners and security allies.

Geopolitically, the globalisation process benefited from the post-Cold War unipolar power structure, with the US as the indisputable centre of geopolitical power. Acting in concert with its allies in Europe and Asia, the US led global power projection. This unipolar situation safeguarded the security structure of sea lanes vital to the global economy – the 'command of the commons'.[8] It also protected the stability of a rules-based framework of trade, finance, and security commitments built during the Cold War years – from GATT/WTO to the IMF, the World Bank and the UN.

The monocentric nexus of geo-economics and geopolitics, and the revolution in information and communication technologies that reduced costs of communication and coordination, created optimal conditions for transnational corporations, especially those from the G7 countries. Firms were able to geographically disperse their production processes via outsourcing and offshoring. Richard Baldwin calls this process globalisation's 'second unbundling'.[9] Transnational corporations established global value-chain networks of production and trade, seeking competitive advantages in new markets in the developing world, particularly in Asia.[10]

This was journalist and author Thomas Friedman's 'flat world', in which the 'globalisation system' replaced the 'Cold War system' as the basic international configuration.[11] Globalisation's monocentric uniformity seemed poised to rule the world. The G7 symbolised this broad fusion between geo-economics and geopolitics. That specific monocentric convergence between geo-economics and geopolitics was somehow perceived as the natural condition of global affairs. So much so that it was easy to be oblivious, as Fareed Zakaria pointed out, that 'the flat economic world has been created by an extremely unflat political world'.[12] It took the 2008 financial crisis to unleash the tectonic shifts in global power recently taking place.

By the end of the 2000s, a structural divergence began to emerge between global geo-economics and geopolitics, subtly decoupling the former from the latter and shaping the power structure of a polycentric globalisation.

A multipolar geo-economic power structure has taken shape in terms of the economic dynamism of production, trade and investments. This decentralisation of economic power does not herald an immediate changing of the guard in global economic power, nor is it a sign of the irrelevance of old power centres. Rather it means that established economic centres such as the US, Europe and Japan now coexist with new centres of economic power – China, India and Brazil, among other emerging economies. In geo-economic multipolarity, diversity becomes the rule.

The unipolar geopolitical power structure is increasingly under pressure from geo-economic transformations and fiscal strains. In geopolitical terms, the US remains the indisputable military power, although other powers are gradually translating their economic success into military, diplomatic and policy capabilities.[13] But, perhaps more importantly, the new geo-economic centres of power are decoupled from the main geopolitical pole of power in terms of security commitments. By implication, economic interdependences no longer perfectly coincide with security arrangements. In the past, this coincidence had real effect. The US–Japan geo-economic competition in the 1980s and the Plaza Agreement in 1985[14] are useful reminders of that condition. Michael Mastanduno recalls that nowadays 'the US dominance in the international security arena no longer translates into effective leverage in the international economic arena'.[15]

The structural match between geo-economics and geopolitics generated uniformity in the globalisation process. Today's structural mismatch is generating multiformity. The process of economic globalisation is taking place within a very different power equilibrium. Debates on the varieties of capitalism, including state capitalism, reflect shifts in the traditional balance of economic power and influence.[16] So do difficulties in concluding the WTO Doha Round trade negotiations and US efforts to negotiate mega-regional trade agreements (mega-RTAs) with Asia-Pacific and the EU.

Negotiating trade: restoring convergence?

Global trade negotiations reflect the structural mismatch between geo-economics and geopolitics. This new reality can be discerned in two important trends:

- Multilaterally, in the tension between the new realities of geo-economic power and the old configuration of power that structured the multilateral trading system over previous rounds of trade negotiations; and
- Regionally, in the US-led mega-RTA negotiations, the Trans-Pacific Partnership (TPP) and the Transatlantic Trade and Investment Partnership (TTIP). These negotiations, while creating tension with the WTO system, seek the double geo-economic goal of: (a) trying to restore the rule-making capacity that was associated with the old monocentric globalisation convergence;[17] and (b) establishing a solid US geo-economic foothold in Eurasia's Pacific Rim and North Atlantic Rim to deal with the rise of China.

The multilateral deadlock in the WTO Doha Round (or Doha Development Agenda) reflects the increasing discrepancy between the major geo-economic transformations of recent years and the international trade regime designed in the age of monocentric globalisation. Launched in 2001, the Doha Round was caught in the middle of a fundamental shift in the global balance of economic power, which has changed the negotiating structure and power dynamics at the WTO.[18]

Reforming and updating the current multilateral trade regime has been the main goal of the Doha Round. The Doha negotiating mandate covers updates in all sectors, including agriculture, manufactured goods and services. Agricultural trade has been central to the negotiations; the sector was insufficiently regulated during the GATT years, and current WTO rules perpetuate decades of trade-distorting policies and practices in developed nations.

Throughout GATT the geo-economic power configuration was clear: the US and Europe were the trade powers and rule-setters of the multilateral trade regime. The so-called WTO Quad of the US, Europe, Japan and Canada formed the decision-making powerhouse of the Uruguay Round, which was finally concluded two years after the pivotal Blair House Agreement between the US and Europe in 1992.[19] But during the WTO Doha Round, new trading powers have emerged. Brazil, China and India have consolidated their position as major trading nations in agriculture, manufactured goods and services respectively. As the *WTR 2013* noted: 'Especially China, but also India and Brazil have transformed the balance of power in the multilateral trading system.'[20] That transformation has changed the negotiating structure, dynamics and the balance of multilateral influence at the WTO.

Established in the post-Cold War era, the WTO is a special institutional case because its decision-making structure is flexible enough to immediately fold geo-economic transformations into the multilateral negotiations. The Uruguay Round Quad was superseded by the Doha Round Quint (Brazil, China, the EU, India and the US). The role and weight of those new powers, and the coalitions they built tilted the balance of rule-making at the WTO.

The central substantive impasse in the Doha Round since 2008 has been about the appropriate balance between agriculture and industrial goods (known as non-agricultural market access, or NAMA), trade reform and liberalisation. Discussions over trade-offs and the overall level of ambition of the negotiations have produced modest progress since 2008. A US-led coalition favours a higher level of ambition in NAMA and services, while developing nations consider it vital to conclude the business of agricultural trade reforms.

At the WTO Ministerial Conference held in Bali in December 2013, incremental steps were taken and a positive deal was reached on issues such as trade facilitation (removing obstacles to the movement of goods across borders, in particular regarding customs procedures and transparency) and agricultural tariff rate quota administration (seeking more transparency and efficiency in national customs management of imports of agricultural goods). The agreement in Bali may build momentum in the negotiations and help to address the central substantive impasses at the heart of the Doha Round, the balance between agriculture and NAMA.

Two different conceptions of the Doha Round objectives have taken shape since 2008. One emphasises the reform and updating of current rules by levelling the playing field and redressing past in-built privileges within the multilateral trade regime. The other seeks to prepare for the future and to hedge the emergence of new trading powers through a harmonisation and parity of commitments between industrialised and emerging nations.

However, these objectives are now being pursued in a different context of power relations. The process of reforming the trade regime has moved from the monocentric geo-economic world of previous GATT negotiation rounds to the polycentric geo-economic world populated by emerging trading powers. Today, negotiations for reforming multilateral rules take place amid an increasingly even balance of economic power and interests. Overcoming the Doha Round impasse will require substantive compromises in favour of preserving the multilateral trading system.

Against this backdrop of multilateral deadlock and power-balance shifts, inter-regional trade agreements are being negotiated, such as the TPP and the Transatlantic Trade and Investment Partnership TTIP. These US-led mega-RTA initiatives are central to Washington's strategy of seeking to regain its pre-eminence in trade rule-making. The revival of the 'competitive liberalisation' debate in US trade policy and the perception of a rising China have also pushed developments in the direction of inter-regional trade negotiations.

The proposed TTIP between the US and EU would bring two major geo-economic forces together in a bloc accounting for 45% of world GDP and 30% of global trade. Tariffs are already low between the two economies, except for agriculture, where, despite US competitiveness in some products, both have an interest to protect. Consequently, the TTIP would fundamentally seek to improve on regulatory and rules issues, as well as the facilitation of investment flows.

The TPP is a very complex negotiation.[21] It involves traditional issues of market access – agriculture, industrial goods and services – and new issues known as WTO-plus and WTO-extra regulations. These include disciplines on state-owned enterprises, intellectual property rights, regulatory coherence, competition policies, rules on investment, e-commerce, supply-chain competitiveness, sanitary and phytosanitary standards and labour and environmental rules.

The TTIP and the TPP are therefore much more than traditional free-trade agreements. They are also offshore agreements, regulating investment and standards beyond borders and creating a favourable business environment for the activities of transnational corporations and their global value chains within the countries involved. These trade agreements ultimately aim to lock in deeper rules and disciplines. If concluded, they will enhance the trading power of existing headquarter economies, namely the US, Germany and Japan. This trend will also reinforce a move towards 'selective liberalism' in sectors that interest headquarter economies' GVCs, leaving unreformed traditionally protected sectors in those headquarter economies, particularly, but not exclusively, in agricultural trade and disciplines.[22]

Political scientist Ashley J. Tellis argues that the US geo-economic strategy should continue to push those mega-regional trade agreements forward, as they have 'the advantage of specifically excluding China' and consequentially 'provide Washington with improved relative gains vis-à-vis Beijing, the *sine qua non* for maintaining US primacy in a competitive international system'.[23]

But the exclusion of China could represent a setback because of its central position in global value chains and the complex regional and inter-regional interdependencies that China's economy has created in Asia and elsewhere in the world. For its part, China is pragmatically keeping its options open, especially because, as the WTO accession process illustrates, international rules can be a powerful tool for domestic reforms. There has been growing public debate in China about the advantages and disadvantages of joining the TPP negotiations.[24] China supported the negotiations launched in 2012 for a Regional Comprehensive Economic Partnership (RCEP) between ASEAN and Australia, China, India, Japan, Korea and New Zealand. More recently, China has suggested the creation of a 'new Pacific free-trade zone' under the auspices of the Asia-Pacific Economic Cooperation (APEC) forum – which includes all TPP countries plus China.[25]

From a geo-economic perspective, both TPP and TTIP negotiations are difficult and complex. The TTIP involves two major trading powers (the US and EU) in a more symmetric economic-power relationship and with high levels of regulatory standards that need to be reconciled. The TPP involves several economies in an asymmetric economic-power relationship and with different levels of regulatory standards that need to be upgraded to the US level. But whatever the negotiating difficulties, a successful conclusion of those mega-RTAs should not be dismissed. Such an outcome would put enormous pressure on the new geo-economic powers and on the multilateral trading system under the WTO. 'Whose trade rules become the norm?' would become the central political question.

Conclusion

'Economic activity is a source of power as well as well-being,' Samuel Huntington wrote in 1993. 'It is indeed probably the most important source of power.'[26] International trade has contributed to important changes in the global geo-economic landscape. Geo-economic centres of power have risen in the past 20 years and now coexist with traditional geo-economic powers. The international power equilibrium that shaped globalisation has been transformed, with the gradual drifting apart of the alignment between geo-economics and geopolitics. Those changes have profoundly impacted global trade negotiations.

In this emerging polycentric structure of globalisation, two interrelated geo-economic trends should be closely observed, given their systemic impacts on international trade. The first is the risk of fragmentation, when the trading system needs cohesion and universality. The geo-economic strategies of major trading powers seem to prioritise the negotiations of inter-regional preferential trade agreements (PTAs). The challenges for the multilateral trade regime are not trivial. New inter-regional PTAs (aka mega-RTAs) could spawn domestic regulations beyond the WTO disciplines and generate trade opening outside the WTO's purview. Regulatory misalignments between regional and multilateral trade rules may divert trade flows and impose costs on the operation of global supply chains.

Mega-regional agreements such as the TPP and the TTIP do not involve only tariffs but are essentially about new regulation of trade-related issues (as described above). Trade regulation may start to move towards WTO-plus and WTO-extra rules. As a consequence, the WTO risks gradually losing its position as the ceiling of the multilateral trade regime and instead becoming its regulatory floor amid a likely proliferation of blocs of regional and inter-regional trade agreements. The worst scenario for international trade and business activities is one of competing trade regionalisms with weakening multilateralism.

The second trend is the exclusion of new trading powers, when they need to be fully integrated into the global trading system. Proponents see two advantages in the mega-RTAs: the possibility of regaining the rule-making initiative and shaping the rules of global trade without having to negotiate with emerging powers; and the future possibility of 'multilateralising' those agreements at the WTO. This assumes, of course, that mega-RTAs will come to fruition at their original level of ambition, which is still uncertain. It also assumes that the multilateralisation of those mega-RTAs will be somehow easier than concluding the Doha Round.

As Richard Baldwin has recently pointed out, while 'some emerging markets – China, India and Brazil – are large enough to attract foreign investment and technology without signing deep RTAs', the risk is that 'by the time their multinationals are ready to make major outward pushes, the rules-of-the-road will have been written by the US, EU and Japan (*sic*) deep RTAs'.[27]

As polycentric globalisation takes shape, reinforcing the centrality of the WTO in the international trade regime remains vital. The more symmetric distribution of geo-economic power at the WTO brings forth a more equal balance among established and rising trade powers. Multilateral negotiations today are much more complex and time-consuming, as the Doha deadlock exemplifies. Asymmetries of power in trade negotiations can more easily be deployed at RTA negotiations. But in the end there are no shortcuts in trying to reach a legitimate international economic order, one that truly reflects the emerging multipolarity of global geo-economics.

Notes

1 Jeffrey Sachs, 'International Economics: Unlocking the Mysteries of Globalisation', *Foreign Policy*, no. 110, Spring 1998.

2 Kevin H. O'Rourke, 'Politics and Trade: Lessons from Past Globalisations', Bruegel Essay and Lecture Series, 2009, p. 8; and Ronald Findlay and Kevin H. O'Rourke, *Power and Plenty: Trade, War, and the World Economy in the Second Millennium* (Princeton, NJ: Princeton University Press, 2007).

3 Kenneth Waltz, 'Globalisation and American Power', *National Interest*, no. 59, Spring 2000, p. 53.

4 *World Trade Report 2013 – Factors Shaping the Future of World Trade* (Geneva: World Trade Organisation, 2013).

5 *Ibid*.

6 Richard Baldwin, 'Global supply chains: why they emerged, why they matter, and where they are going', in Deborah K. Elms and Patrick Low (eds), *Global Value Chains in a Changing World* (Geneva: World Trade Organisation, 2013).

7 Richard Baldwin, 'WTO 2.0: Global Governance of Supply-Chain Trade', *CEPR Policy Insight*, no. 64, December 2012, p. 5.

8 Barry R. Posen, 'Command of the Commons: The Military Foundation of US Hegemony', *International Security*, vol. 28, no. 1 (Summer 2003), pp. 5–46.

9 Richard Baldwin, 'Globalisation: the great unbundling(s)', Paper forming part of the Globalisation Challenges for Europe and Finland project, Economic Council of Finland, 2006.

10 Transnational corporations' global production networks are mainly formed in specific manufacturing industries, e.g., electronics, automotive, machinery, textiles, chemicals and plastics. Extractive and service industries tag on GVCs providing inputs for many other industries' exports. It is important to observe that, as transnational corporations have shaped GVCs, their strategies can also restructure them. New technologies may impact GVCs (e.g., 3D printing and computer-integrated manufacturing) and create the conditions for 'reshoring' tasks and functions performed abroad. Labour and energy costs may also affect GVCs' competitiveness (e.g., rising manufacturing costs in 'Factory Asia' and the shale-gas revolution in the US). Those changes would certainly affect current geo-economic interdependences among countries involved in GVCs and generate new geo-economic risks.

11 Thomas L. Friedman, *The Lexus and the Olive Tree* (New York: Farrar, Straus & Giroux, 1999); and *The World Is Flat* (New York: Farrar, Straus & Giroux, 2005).

12 Fareed Zakaria, 'The World is Flat: The Wealth of Yet More Nations', *New York Times,* 1 May 2005.

13 The IISS 2014 *Military Balance*, for instance, estimates that the US 2013 defence budget of US$600bn is only slightly smaller than the other top 15 countries' defence budgets combined. China has the second-highest defence budget (US$112bn), followed by Russia (US$68bn); see *The Military Balance 2014* (Abingdon: Routledge for the IISS, 2014), p. 23.

14 With the Plaza Agreement signed by 'G5' nations (the US, Japan, West Germany, Britain and France) at the Plaza Hotel in New York City in 1985, the US dollar was depreciated relative to the German Deutschmark and the Japanese Yen. The agreement effectively acted as a boost to US exports.

15 Michael Mastanduno, 'System Maker and Privilege Taker: US Power and the International Political Economy', *World Politics,* vol. 61, no. 1, January 2009, p. 123.

16 See Ian Bremmer, 'The Return of State Capitalism', *Survival: Global Politics and Strategy*, vol. 50, no. 3, June–July 2008, pp. 55–64; and Aldo Musacchio and Sergio Lazzarini, 'Leviathan in Business: Varieties of State Capitalism and their Implications for Economic Performance', Harvard Business School, Working Paper 12–108 (June 2012).

17 Charles Kupchan, for instance, sees the TTIP as an opportunity to revitalise the West's position as the anchor of a liberal order amid changes in world power; see Charles A. Kupchan, 'Parsing TTIP's Geopolitical Implications', Transatlantic Partnership Forum Working Paper Series (June 2014).

18 The argument that the Doha Round deadlock is predominantly a function of the structural changes in the global balance of power is put forward by Braz Baracuhy, 'Rising Powers, Reforming Challenges', Centre for Rising Powers, Cambridge University, Working Paper No. 1, May 2011; Guy de Jonquières, 'The Multilateralism Conundrum: International Economic Relations in the Post-hegemonic Era', European Centre for International Political Economy (ECIPE), Transatlantic Task Force on Trade Working Paper No. 1 (2011); and Pascal Lamy, 'Putting Geopolitics Back at the Trade Table', Speech at the IISS–Oberoi Discussion Forum, New Delhi, India, 29 January 2013.

19 The 1992 Blair House Accord was an agreement between the US and EU to reduce agricultural subsidies to exporters and domestic producers.

20 *WTR 2013*, p. 286.

21 See Glossary.

22 GVCs and selective liberalism are discussed in George de Oliveira Marques, 'Global Value Chains: International Trade's "New Narrative" and its Implications for Brazil' (Mimeo, 2014).

23 Ashley J. Tellis, 'Balancing without Containment: A US Strategy for Confronting China's Rise', *Washington Quarterly*, Fall 2013, pp. 114–15.

24 Zhang Maorong, 'China could have key role to play in TPP', *Global Times*, 20 November 2013.

25 Bob Davis, 'China Pushes its New Pacific Free-Trade Zone at APEC Meeting', *Wall Street Journal*, 18 May 2014.

26 Samuel P. Huntington, 'Why International Primacy Matters', *International Security*, vol. 17, no. 4, Spring 1993, p. 72.

27 Richard Baldwin, 'Globalisation, global supply chains and the implications of megaregionalism', Paper presented at the IISS Geo-economics and Strategy Programme's conference 'Trade and Flag: The Changing Balance of Power in the Multilateral Trading System' (Mimeo), IISS–Middle East, Bahrain, 6–8 April 2014.

Economic shocks and the geo-economics of world trade

Sanjaya Baru and Suvi Dogra

Among the many important lessons of the twentieth centu-ry's Great Depression and the economic crises of the interwar years was the understanding that competitive 'beggar-my-neighbour' policies had accelerated a race to the bottom of all competing economies rather than promoted the national economic growth of any.[1] A direct consequence of that learning was the decision by many countries, led by the victors of the Second World War, to create multilateral economic institutions that would define and enforce global 'rules of the game'. The Bretton Woods system, defined by the International Monetary Fund and the World Bank and its affiliates, did not quite consti-tute the 'world government' that economist John Maynard Keynes had wished to see, but it defined certain rules of the global economic and financial system.[2]

On a parallel track, some United Nations member states came together to create a new global trading order under the aegis of an International Trade Organisation (ITO), created in 1947. But the ITO never really took off and was wound up by

1950.[3] An attempt was then made to define the rules of world trade via a General Agreement on Tariffs and Trade (GATT) entered into by just 23 nations.

As signatories to GATT increased, this plurilateral agreement defined the world trading order for nearly half a century.[4] As Ashley J. Tellis observes in this volume, 'GATT was an American-led enterprise that sought an orderly, reciprocal and multilateral reduction in tariffs, and provided the foundations upon which a liberal international economic order, despite numerous imperfections, could gradually grow.'[5]

It is a testament to the growing complexity of the global power system, and to the growth in the number of sovereign members, that while the first round of GATT negotiations, called the Geneva Round, between 23 contracting parties, was completed in 1947 in only seven months, the eighth round, called the Uruguay Round, between 123 contracting parties, took 91 months.[6] Indeed, the first five rounds of GATT negotiations – Geneva (1947), Annecy (1949), Torquay (1950), Geneva-II (1956) and Dillon (1960) – were all wound up within the year. Most finished in five or six months, with only the Dillon Round stretching up to 11. Because of an increase in the number of nations involved from 26 to 62, and on account of the wider agenda of trade liberalisation, the Kennedy Round launched in 1965 took close to three years to be negotiated. The Tokyo Round, launched in 1973, took 67 months.[7]

By the time the Uruguay Round was launched in 1986 the world had changed significantly. Not only had 123 countries entered the negotiating process, but a new group of emerging economies, especially East Asia's export-oriented economies, had also begun to assert their interests in defining the global rules. Finally, even as the Uruguay Round finally gained traction the geopolitical parameters defining the multilateral economic system changed. Within four years of the round's launch, the Cold War ended, the Soviet Union collapsed and global power equations were radically redefined.

This had a paradoxical impact on GATT. On the one hand, developed market economies became even more ambitious in their desire to create a more open global trading system. On the other hand, both developed and many developing nations wanted a more predictable trading environment with rules that would and could be enforced, and that would guard against non-tariff forms of protection. Thus, while the Uruguay Round dragged on, one of its key deliverables became the replacement of GATT with a new version of the aborted ITO. This institutional mechanism to implement GATT, now called the World Trade Organisation (WTO), was to be equipped with more effective mechanisms to address and resolve disputes among members.

The WTO and the Uruguay Round agreement were crafted amid the end of the Cold War and during what geopolitical analysts refer to as, the 'unipolar moment'.[8] Critics of the Uruguay Round expressed dismay at the fact that the multilateral trading system was now shaping what they saw as non-trade related policy, including intellectual property rights protection. Concerned by the further push to include new issues like labour, social and environment policies in the rules for global trade, developing countries united to define the new round of trade negotiations launched in 2000 in Qatar as the 'Doha Round' or the 'Doha Development Agenda' (DDA), depending upon one's preferred nomenclature. The word 'development' was specifically included to underline developing countries' concerns. Clearly the 'unipolar moment' had passed and in the emerging 'multipolar world' rising trade powers like China, Brazil and India began to assert their interests.

In the two decades since its 1995 launch, the WTO has succeeded in creating a new global regime for trade, not just in goods but also in services – and many developing countries are seeking the inclusion of the movement of people across borders in the WTO's ambit. The essays in this volume offer a fair summary of the many successes of GATT and the WTO. Indeed, from this success has emerged a problem. The creators of the GATT/WTO system feel increasingly challenged by newly emerging exporting powers, especially China. Many of the essays in this volume draw attention to the fact that the emergence of China as a global 'mega-trader' has forced several developed economies to reassess their approach to free trade and multilateralism. The competitive challenge posed by emerging powers has also compelled many global trade players to pursue regional/preferential trade agreements, which by nature discriminate against non-members.

Alongside growing support for protectionist policies in the developed world from various lobbies, several policymakers have shown their preference for new plurilateral trading arrangements that many developing countries view as the thin end of the wedge of protectionism and a departure from the deadlocked Doha Round of negotiations. While the WTO charter allows for regional, preferential and plurilateral trade associations to coexist, and hundreds have come into being, the two initiatives undertaken by the US administration in the aftermath of the transatlantic financial and economic crisis of 2008–09 have raised particular doubts about the future of the multilateral system under the WTO.

While the idea of a Trans-Pacific Partnership (TPP) was floated by some Pacific countries even before the 2008 crisis, it gained traction within the US after the crisis and against the background of US concerns about the trade and capital-account 'imbalances' vis-à-vis China. Soon afterwards, the US and EU initiated talks on a Transatlantic Trade and Investment Partnership (TTIP). Against this background, Edward

Luttwak's assertion that China's economic rise would 'inevitably be resisted by geo-economic means' including 'strategically motivated trade barriers' encouraged many to view these initiatives as designed to secure the 'geo-economic containment' of China.[9]

Defenders of the TPP and TTIP, on the other hand, view them as 'WTO-plus' treaties, a gold standard for trade agreements; and this view will be reinforced if the initiatives successfully resolve disagreements in difficult areas such as agriculture and cross-border rules in services and investments, thereby enabling a coalition of willing economies to break out of the impasse in DDA created by a similar coalition of developing countries with very different policy priorities.

A third, and more important, argument in defence of TPP- and TTIP-style plurilateralism is the argument based on the changing structure of global manufacturing. In a paper presented at an IISS Geo-economics and Strategy Programme Conference, 'Trade and Flag', trade economist Richard Baldwin suggests that moves to create new WTO-plus plurilateral trading regimes are being driven by fundamental structural changes in global manufacturing, with international trade no longer an exchange of goods and services between nations but increasingly intra-firm trade based on global value chains (GVCs).[10] Trade is no longer about cross-border flows of finished goods or even components, but also includes the cross-border movement of ideas, technology, people and all other elements involved in production and distribution processes.

Baldwin says 'trade – as traditionally conceived – involves the competition between national teams of labour, capital, know-how, institutions, etc. With GVCs, we are seeing large corporations mixing and matching labour, capital and know-how from several nations. One should no longer think of Mercedes versus Lexus as a German team competing with a

Japanese team. Both corporations are leveraging their firm-specific know-how by organising international production networks in search of ever better quality–cost ratios. Quite simply, the traditional sources of national comparative advantage are on the move inside international production networks. The key technology boundaries these days are the boundary of GVC lead firms, not the boundaries of specific nations.'[11]

Based on this view of trade, several economists have defended plurilateral trade initiatives as business-led policy frameworks aimed at increasing the efficiency of global manufacturing. In remarks on the Bhagwati, Krishna and Panagariya paper in this volume (see Chapter One), Deborah Elms says that the TPP would facilitate not just duty-free movement of goods within firms across borders, but also businesses-services liberalisation. Says Elms, 'Since up to half the value in a chain may be composed of services, this is also a key element for business in the twenty-first century. This new agreement will also free up and protect investment in participating countries. It provides faster trade facilitation, improved intellectual property rights protection, better dispute settlement mechanisms and more.'[12] She believes the TTIP would offer similar benefits to firms. 'The TTIP is aiming at harmonising rules and standards. Since these are a principal barrier to firms today, minimising these impediments to trade could unleash whole new areas of growth between Europe and the United States.'[13]

Clearly, these are the three contending world views on plurilateral trade agreements: 1) that they run parallel to the WTO but offer fast-track liberalisation of trade for countries willing to run faster, and that they offer a way out of the impasse in the WTO's Doha Round; 2) that they are in fact not WTO-plus but a way out of the WTO to facilitate the geo-economic containment of the new mega-trader, China; and 3) that they are a response to structural changes in global manufacturing with the spread of cross-border intra-firm links through global value chains and supply-chain networks.

Depending on where one is situated in the global economy, therefore, the emergence of mega-regional trade agreements (mega-RTAs) appears as either a positive or negative trend, as either opportunity or threat, or as a trade creator or trade diverter.

The papers presented in this volume reiterate the view that strengthening and preserving the multilateral trading order under the aegis of the WTO is important, necessary and valuable from the viewpoint of both development and global economic growth. While recognising the appeal of mega-RTAs to global corporations, we adopt the view that the world would be better off with regulatory convergence, with all economies moving towards commonly acceptable global norms, rather than with a new trade war between the established trading powers, the US and EU, and new mega-trader China, or with a continuation of the *ancien régime* of US–EU dominance.

Such a consensual outcome requires, however, progress on the Doha Development Agenda. It calls for compromise on the part of all concerned, developed and developing. It is a measure of the nature of geopolitical change in the world, of the power shift from the West to the rest, that few worry about the possibility of the US trying to undo the multilateral GATT/WTO system it created just because that system no longer suits its interests.[14] When, for example, India decided to walk away from the Bali consensus on trade facilitation, demanding reassurance over provisions for food subsidy in the agreement on agriculture,[15] there were concerted attempts afterwards to arrive at an outcome that would satisfy all. This points to a desire among both developed and developing economies to preserve the existing multilateral trading system, whatever its inadequacies.

It remains to be seen whether the US and EU could disman-
tle a multilateral trading regime they are no longer happy
with, and erect one that suits their interests, in defiance of the
interests of developing economies, especially a mega-trader
like China. The ability of the US to seek the geo-economic
containment of China through new plurilateral arrangements
is equally uncertain. What is clear, however, is that increased
and growing cross-border integration of manufacturing and
services has made it necessary for all economies to eliminate
barriers to trade. Developing countries seek a supportive
playing field, not just a level one, and a widening of the trade
agenda to include the movement of people and not just of
goods, services, investments and capital.

Does this mean that bilateral and regional trade agreements
should give way to multilateralism? The answer is no. On the
long road to achieving inclusive global governance under the
larger umbrella of multilateralism, there is a need for multilateral trade agreements such as the TPP and TTIP, and for
regional multilateral organisations such as ASEAN that can
address the concerns of participants at a local level. Ultimately,
these serve to strengthen the current multilateral institutions
or as a launch pad to create new ones that do not inherit the
democratic deficits that inflict the current set-ups.

Multilateralism is not an end in and of itself. The existing infrastructure and procedures of global governance have
struggled to accommodate new players in the shifting power
landscape of the twenty-first century, and the playing field
is far from level. That said, the way to transform or upgrade
the multilateral system, and to do away with the disenchantment towards the WTO, may not involve an either/or choice
between the current multilateral powerhouses and the active
new forces of the global order, but an amalgamation of both.[16]
Regionalism is sufficiently entrenched in the global trade envi-

ronment to enthral new members. Therefore, the challenge for an institution such as the WTO is to ensure that the new trade agreements are compatible with the larger goal of global free trade.

Strengthening multilateral institutions and regimes is vital, and the Doha Development Round must be brought to a successful conclusion, irrespective of what happens with parallel plurilateral agreements. It is in the interests of the global economy that the WTO is strengthened and given a new lease of life by bringing to a successful closure the first round of trade negotiations conducted under its auspices.

Notes

[1] See Robert Skidelsky, 'Keynes, Globalisation and the Bretton Woods Institutions in the Light of Changing Ideas about Market', *World Economics*, vol. 6, no. 1, November 2004.

[2] Robert Skidelsky, *Keynes: The Return of the Master* (London: Allen Lane, 2009), chapter 5.

[3] 'The GATT Years: From Havana to Marrakesh', World Trade Organisation, Geneva, http://www.wto.org/English/thewto_e/whatis_e/tif_e/fact4_e.htm.

[4] *Ibid.*

[5] Ashley J. Tellis, Chapter Six, this volume.

[6] From September 1986 to April 1994, see http://www.wto.org/english/thewto_e/whatis_e/tif_e/fact5_e.htm.

[7] From September 1973 to April 1979, see http://worldtradereview.com/webpage.asp?wID=438.

[8] Charles Krauthammer, 'The Unipolar Moment Revisted', *National Interest*, Winter 2002–03, http://belfercenter.ksg.harvard.edu/files/krauthammer.pdf.

[9] Edward Luttwak, *The Rise of China vs. The Logic of Strategy* (Cambridge, MA: The Belknap Press of Harvard University Press, 2012), p. 42.

[10] Richard Baldwin, 'Globalisation, global supply chains and the implications of megaregionalism', Paper presented at the IISS Geo-economics and Strategy Programme's conference 'Trade and Flag: The Changing Balance of Power in the Multilateral Trading System' (Mimeo), IISS–Middle East, Bahrain, 6–8 April 2014.

[11] *Ibid.*

[12] Deborah K. Elms, 'Comment on the Bhagwati, Krishna and Panagariya Paper', IISS 'Trade and Flag' Conference (Mimeo).

[13] *Ibid.*

[14] On the idea of global 'power shifts' and the role of 'economic shocks', see Sanjaya Baru, 'Understanding

Geo-economics and Strategy', *Survival: Global Politics and Strategy*, vol. 54, no. 3, June–July 2012.

[15] In Bali in December 2013, members of the WTO, including India, agreed to a trade facilitation agreement (TFA) to simplify customs procedures. However, India pulled out of the TFA shortly before it was due to be ratified in July 2014 due to other concerns over the WTO rule that caps subsidies to farmers in developing countries at 10% of the total value of agricultural production, based on 1986–88 prices. Developing countries argue that the base year is now outdated and they need room to stock enough edible grains for the food security of millions of their poor. India was particularly concerned because the minimum support price it pays to farmers under a new US$4bn-a-year scheme to supply cheap food to 800m people could lead it to breach the 10% cap. The 2013 Bali Ministerial Conference discussed a 'peace clause' provisionally shielding public stockholding programmes for food security in developing countries from legal challenges for four years. However, India was not reassured by this, and the deadlock was only overcome in November 2014, when a firmer 'peace clause' was agreed.

[16] For a detailed understanding of traditional types of multilateralism see Robert Cox, 'Multilateralism and World Order', *Review of International Studies*, vol. 18, no. 2, April 1992, pp. 161–80.

INDEX

Adelphi books are published eight times a year by Routledge Journals, an imprint of Taylor & Francis, 4 Park Square, Milton Park, Abingdon, Oxfordshire OX14 4RN, UK.

A subscription to the institution print edition, ISSN 1944-5571, includes free access for any number of concurrent users across a local area network to the online edition, ISSN 1944-558X. Taylor & Francis has a flexible approach to subscriptions enabling us to match individual libraries' requirements. This journal is available via a traditional institutional subscription (either print with free online access, or online-only at a discount) or as part of the Strategic, Defence and Security Studies subject package or Strategic, Defence and Security Studies full text package. For more information on our sales packages please visit www.tandfonline.com/librarians_pricinginfo_journals.

2015 Annual Adelphi Subscription Rates			
Institution	£615	$1,079 USD	€910
Individual	£217	$371 USD	€296
Online only	£538	$944 USD	€796

Dollar rates apply to subscribers outside Europe. Euro rates apply to all subscribers in Europe except the UK and the Republic of Ireland where the pound sterling price applies. All subscriptions are payable in advance and all rates include postage. Journals are sent by air to the USA, Canada, Mexico, India, Japan and Australasia. Subscriptions are entered on an annual basis, i.e. January to December. Payment may be made by sterling cheque, dollar cheque, international money order, National Giro, or credit card (Amex, Visa, Mastercard).

For a complete and up-to-date guide to Taylor & Francis journals and books publishing programmes, and details of advertising in our journals, visit our website: **http://www.tandfonline.com.**

Ordering information:
USA/Canada: Taylor & Francis Inc., Journals Department, 325 Chestnut Street, 8th Floor, Philadelphia, PA 19106, USA. **UK/Europe/Rest of World:** Routledge Journals, T&F Customer Services, T&F Informa UK Ltd., Sheepen Place, Colchester, Essex, CO3 3LP, UK.

Advertising enquiries to:
USA/Canada: The Advertising Manager, Taylor & Francis Inc., 325 Chestnut Street, 8th Floor, Philadelphia, PA 19106, USA. Tel: +1 (800) 354 1420. Fax: +1 (215) 625 2940. **UK/Europe/Rest of World**: The Advertising Manager, Routledge Journals, Taylor & Francis, 4 Park Square, Milton Park, Abingdon, Oxfordshire OX14 4RN, UK. Tel: +44 (0) 20 7017 6000. Fax: +44 (0) 20 7017 6336.

The print edition of this journal is printed on ANSI conforming acid-free paper by Bell & Bain, Glasgow, UK.